LUTHER AND LIBERATION

LUTHER AND LIBERATION

A Latin American Perspective

WALTER ALTMANN

Translated by Mary M. Solberg

Wipf and Stock Publishers
150 West Broadway • Eugene OR 97401
2000

to Madalena,
who with encouragement and concern
assisted at the birth of these perceptions and thoughts,
so often at odd hours of the day and night . . .

LUTHER AND LIBERATION:
A Latin American Perspective

This volume is based on Walter Altmann, *Confrontación y liberación: Una perspectiva latinoamericana sobre Martín Lutero*, published in 1987 by ISEDET, Buenos Aires, Argentina. Copyright © 1987 Asociación Interconfesional de Estudios Teológicos.

Scripture quotations are from the New Revised Standard Version Bible, copyright © 1989 by the Division of Christian Education of the National Council of the Churches of Christ in the United States of America. Used with permission.

Interior design: Karen Buck
Cover design: Hilber Nelson

Luther and Liberation
A Latin American Perspective
By Altmann, Walter
Copyright©1992 by Augsburg Fortress
ISBN: 1-57910-548-3

Reprinted by *Wipf and Stock Publishers*
150 West Broadway • Eugene OR 97401

Previously published by Augsburg Fortress, 1992.

Contents

Preface

I have never been able to read Martin Luther at a distance. Of course, he lived five centuries ago in a totally different context. Nevertheless, the type of presumptuous scientific objectivity that leads either to cold neutrality or to uncritical repetition of Luther's assertions was never possible for me and, in fact, could never attract me.

This is true in part because the way I approach theology, coming from my Latin American experience, does not allow a sense of uncommitted distance. There is almost a full consensus among Latin American theologians that we always approach theology as affected people—affected by our past experience and history, by our social setting, and by our living faith commitment. When we read Luther's writings, we are always confronted by them in a very peculiar way, which we might share to some extent—yet never fully—with others whose experiences, situations, convictions, and views are similar.

For the sake of our own credibility, then, it is strongly advisable—even essential—that we acknowledge to ourselves and others the context and perspective out of which we approach theology. So let me advise the reader from the very beginning: This book is a Latin American reading of Luther's theology, with all that statement implies. This reminder is perhaps unnecessary, because it will become evident throughout the book. It is, however, appropriate to recall that this has not been done as a free choice but out of fundamental methodological and hermeneutical considerations.

The other reason that I am not able to deal with Luther's writings at a cool and comfortable distance lies in Luther and his writings themselves. Caught in the midst of dramatic, transitional events for the church and, indeed, for the Western world, Luther acted and reacted in what he thought were relevant and necessary ways, in response to the signs of the times and to the Word of God. He did not have the leisure—not even when confined to the Wartburg—nor did he perceive it as either desirable or possible, to retreat into "neutral" objectivity. It always is clear immediately which side he stood on. His writings make claims that go far beyond the terms of an intellectual dispute, to encompass the life and death options facing those who are struggling with the challenges. I have difficulty with those descriptions of Luther's theology that may do justice to Luther's words but not to the context in which they were said or written or to the basic claim inherent in them.

Most of the time, I find Luther's writings fascinating; once in a while, they are also irritating. If he still can have this impact after five centuries and across oceans, in the midst of different cultures, and in radically different church situations, what must Luther's impact have been in his own time? This book attempts to address the issue of his impact in his own time and in ours. Of course, the latter discussion must not be at the expense of an equally necessary effort at objectivity. On the contrary, the clear recognition of the conditions in which and the presuppositions out of which we approach theology is integral to the only form of objectivity that is possible—one of open dialogue between Luther and us today. Otherwise, we might keep our presuppositions and basic assumptions hidden and, what is worse, run the risk of convincing ourselves and trying to convince others that Luther meant to say what we assume from the beginning but fail to acknowledge.

Therefore, the reader should not be surprised to find leaps in time throughout the book. Often, I outline a problem that is significant for the Christian faith today, in particular in the Latin American context; next, I address Luther's views on that particular subject; and finally, I comment on the relevance of these views for the previously outlined situation. The contrast between then and now in itself might reveal a good deal of Luther's relevance for the present. Often, however, radical changes must also be recognized and developed. The one Gospel is not preserved by the mere repetition of the wording but rather by bringing to light this liberating event in the new context, even if this requires major shifts in terminology and concepts.

This method of confronting our questions with Luther's theology in his time could have been superseded by a more historical approach. We could have explored the ways in which Luther's theology developed through the intervening centuries and on different continents.

Such an approach would have involved pursuing the hermeneutical question of the historical effects of Luther's theology. We would then have had to deal very carefully with highly significant questions like this one: Why and how did it happen that so many of Luther's truly revolutionary insights were later domesticated, losing so much of their impact and power, when they were not actually turned into their opposites? How could a radical and uncompromising theology, developed in the midst of life-threatening situations, come in so many instances—as in Nazi Germany, for example—to be abused as a theology of the preservation of the status quo and of full obedience to the state, to arbitrary and atrocious authorities?

Although aware of the problematic they articulate, this book does not pursue these important questions. The discussion that follows assumes that much of Luther's liberating and revolutionary impact has been lost and that it is important to rescue those elements from their captivity. Here, the gap between centuries and situations, and the contrast that arises out of it, might be helpful, too.

Therefore, this book is primarily focused on rescuing Luther's liberating role and insights. On the other hand, Luther did have several darker sides, and they were grave ones. But I am convinced that the Gospel is liberating in a personal and ecclesial, as well as in a social and political sense, and that Luther must be seen in first instance as a witness to this liberating Gospel.

Most of the material in this book is based on research done in 1983, the quincentennial of Luther's birthday. In that year, I was privileged to be invited by the Instituto Superior Evangélico de Estudios Teológicos (ISEDET), in Buenos Aires, Argentina, to give its prestigious Carnahan Lectures as well as a seminar on Luther's positions on some key social-ethical questions. The lectures and the seminar materials, along with two other essays, were later published in Spanish. The English edition has been totally revised. Some parts, which are so bound to specific Latin American situations that their pertinence would hardly be perceived outside that setting, were left out; other sections were added.

The first chapter offers an initial, overall picture of the significance of Luther's theology in his own time and for today. It also addresses the often raised question as to whether Luther should be understood as a late representative of medieval mentality or as a representative of the modern age.

Chapters 2 through 6 are the core of this book. They deal with key issues in Luther's theology: the cross, justification, Scripture, the church, and God's rule in the church and in politics (the so-called two kingdoms doctrine). In these chapters, questions are raised from today's context; then Luther's theology is discussed; finally, the relevance of this theology is suggested.

Chapter 7 deals with specific issues of social, political, and ethical significance. The subjects chosen here are political reform, education, economy, war, resistance, and violence. Originally designed as materials for a seminar discussion format, each section begins with selections from key Luther writings. This approach reflects my experience that Luther's own writings often provide the best springboard, provoking better and more appropriate discussion and leading to creative and challenging insights. The selections in each section are followed by background information, with comments on the writings and occasionally on different positions taken by Luther at various stages of his life. These sections conclude with key questions and reflections intended to motivate readers to their own reflection on Luther's writings and on the topics addressed. The original setting for this chapter explains its colloquial style, as well as the fact that references to other books are generally omitted in this section.

The final chapter addresses the intriguing question of what, after all, is Luther's legacy. It thus closes the circle, returning by a different route to the questions with which the book began. But should the circle of interpretation be closed at all—or should it remain open? To the many images of Luther I may have added one more. The one drawn in this book does not claim to be the "real" Luther or the "true" Luther. It does try to draw a picture that is faithful to the materials we have by and about Luther; at the same time, it does not evade the hermeneutical question of his relevance (and his limitations) for the experience of Christians who long for justice and are willing to struggle for it out of their faith.

Many people, more than I can acknowledge by name, contributed in various ways to the publication of this book. First, I must mention students and faculty colleagues at my own seminary, the Lutheran School of Theology, of the Evangelical Church of the Lutheran Confession in Brazil (in São Leopoldo); at ISEDET (Buenos Aires); and at Luther Northwestern Theological Seminary (St. Paul, Minnesota), where I taught in 1987 to 1988, for their challenging questions, comments, and critique.

I owe special thanks to John Stumme and Mary Solberg. John, currently the Associate Director in the Department of Studies, the Division for Church and Society of the Evangelical Lutheran Church in America (ELCA), was professor of systematic theology at ISEDET in 1983. The publication of this book in Spanish is due in large part to his involvement in preparing and editing the materials. He also urged from the beginning that these materials be made available in English.

I met Mary Solberg in 1986, at a conference on justification and justice that brought together North American and Latin American Lutheran theologians in Mexico City. She had had a transformative experience of Christian involvement in Central America. The following year, as a student at Luther Northwestern, she became my assistant. More than that, she was a challenging dialogue partner. Now she has become the more than capable translator of this book. Her comments and queries, emerging from her experience in both Central America and the United States, greatly enriched my work on the English edition.

Sincere thanks are due also to Fortress Press for including this book in its publication program, and to editor J. Michael West for his interest and his competent and friendly support.

The process of a book's birth reminds the author of Paul's insight that we are but members of one body and, as such, are indebted to the other members.

Walter Altmann
Escola Superior de Teología
São Leopoldo, Brazil

1

Luther at the Juncture of the Old and the New

Luther's importance in his own time and his relevance for ours are too evident for us to ignore. Yet nothing is more inappropriate than honoring Luther, who described himself at the end of his life as "a poor stinking bag of worms." One of the altar paintings by Lucas Cranach the Elder in the church of Wittenberg illustrates Luther's self-understanding. In the pulpit, preaching to the gathered community, Luther points to Jesus on the cross. Luther found his worth in being God's instrument, proclaiming the Savior, the expression of the incommensurable love of God for humanity. Honoring Luther carries with it then an objective risk—that of inverting Luther's own view of himself as a mere witness to the gospel.

If we pay attention to the person and the work of Luther, it also becomes clear that attempts to portray him as a hero are entirely misguided. His theology, far from being a systematic and linear work, is more like a continuous response, often with unforeseen twists and turns, to an endless stream of challenges and problems. He generated neither terminological uniformity nor unchangeable positions.

As a person, too, Luther contradicts the image of a hero. There were moments in his life when he demonstrated extraordinary courage. His defiant shout of No! at the Diet at Worms in 1521, which challenged political power in the name of the gospel, is the best known example. He then had to live the rest of his life as an outlaw. And in 1527, when the plague began to decimate the population of Wittenberg, he refused his prince's request to leave the city. As a priest, he said, his place was at the side of the sick and dying.

Luther was also a person who experienced frequent and profound emotional distress. Often physically ill, he had to comfort himself in

1

his own weakness. He was a deeply troubled person; he often felt the distresses of an anxious conscience and a broken heart. Existential doubts tormented him. In the midst of life, he repeatedly encountered fear of death. At such times he could not find reserves of energy within himself. He could only "cry out in prayer" and remember that he had been baptized—accepted by God.

Finally, we cannot take pride in all Luther's positions; on the contrary, we should be ashamed of some of them. An irascible human being, he did sometimes concede his excesses—often slanderous—in accusing his adversaries. The epithet "ass" applied by Luther to the pope was doubtless very tame; "spoon of snot" is surely a better example of his lexical creativity.

A number of his positions with respect to specific groups of people were more tragic. After having defended the Jews during the first years of the Reformation, for example, his disappointment at their failure to convert to the evangelical cause drove Luther toward the end of his life to incite both the common people and the authorities to violent repression of the Jews. He called for similar persecution of the Anabaptists, a dissident wing of the Reformation. His appeal to the princes to massacre the rebellious peasants is all too well known—or perhaps it has never been known well enough.

We should and can understand the historical circumstances and Luther's subjective feelings in all these instances. But we ought never suggest that these shameful positions were justified. To honor Luther, then, also carries with it the risk of commemorating what cannot be celebrated, of legitimating his errors.

Despite these caveats, there is no question about Luther's positive historical significance. He played an important, even decisive, role in an epoch of cultural, social, political, economic, and religious transition. Living and working at the juncture between the old and the new, Luther made a remarkable contribution toward the emergence of the new, not least of all in three areas: (1) the church and spirituality; (2) the relation between faith and the world; and (3) society, politics, and the economy. First, we will look at Luther in his own time and context, and then ask whether his historic contributions might speak to our own time and place, and if so, how.

The Church and Spirituality

The last centuries of the Middle Ages were already characterized by a deep longing for the reformation of the church. Different ecclesiastical movements, including the monastic and lay movements, even the Renaissance humanism of an Erasmus of Rotterdam, sought to revitalize the church, to rescue it from signs of decadence, to purify it of abuses, to disconnect it from economic interests and political powers. Significantly, the eagerness for the transformation of the church was allied with growing nationalist protests, among them the famous "grievances of the German nation," presented at imperial diets since 1456,[1] against various taxes and obligations toward the church of Rome. Church dignitaries were both feudal lords and wielders of political power. The sale of indulgences that Luther came to oppose was only one link in an intricate chain of tax collection and other oppressive measures.

In the context of Christendom, any reform of society had to occur by way of the reformation of the church. Luther struck a heavy blow when, in his 1520 treatise *To the Christian Nobility of the German Nation Concerning the Reform of the Christian Estate,* he published his proposals for profound economic and social reforms after proposing incisive, radical reforms of the political-religious system.[2]

One of the means by which it was hoped the reform of the church could be realized was a council. In previous centuries, the conciliar movement had been a current antagonistic to the papacy. For some time, Luther placed his hopes in this option, but the Fifth Lateran Council (1512 to 1517) had frustrated this route by reinforcing the centralized power of the hierarchical, papal system. The needed reform had to come in other ways.

In the final centuries of the Middle Ages, another movement also sought the reestablishment of religious truth. This was a movement of personal piety, or mysticism, and it rejected any pretense of institutional church reform. At least it relegated such reform to second place. The necessary spiritual revitalization was sought not through action on external structures but first through the transformation of persons by means of a renewal of faith, religious experience, and piety. Prayer and meditation were the preferred instruments of this path, which had as its destination personal and intimate union with the Savior. Mysticism influenced Luther profoundly.

Luther's discovery of justification by grace through faith took account of both longings simultaneously: the longing for authentic personal faith and the longing for reformation of the church. How? The

---

[1]Franz Lau, *Luther,* translated by Robert H. Fischer (Philadelphia: Westminster Press, 1963), 21.

[2]*Luther's Works,* ed. Jaroslav Pelikan and Helmut T. Lehman (St. Louis: Concordia Publishing House; and Philadelphia: Fortress Press, 1955–), Vol. 44: 123–217. Cited hereafter as *LW.*

doctrine of justification by faith was a profound personal experience of liberation for Luther that had immediate repercussions in both church and society. For Luther, it brought the whole anxious search for salvation, unreachable by means of meritorious works, to an end. Despair gave way to certainty, fear gave way to freedom, the anxious concern for himself was transformed into utter dedication to the rediscovered good news and to the neighbor.

This personal discovery was a kind of response to the longing expressed in mysticism, with one significant advantage: No special, unusual practices were necessary to obtain its blessings. Through faith, blessing was available to all people. The multitudes who flocked to buy indulgences, anxious for the mitigation or annulment of their penalties in purgatory, had no fonder hope than this. The trade in indulgences offered an apparently easy opportunity to "ordinary" Christians, those who could not dedicate themselves to rigorous ascetic practices reserved for members of religious orders. However, the practice was only apparently easy, because it was illusory and steeped in ecclesiastical extortion. Luther's message that there was no easy way— "that the whole life of the believer should be penitence"[3]—but that by the mercy of God and the death of Jesus Christ, salvation was granted freely to those who believe, spread like wildfire. It was explosive liberation not only for Luther but for a whole people.

This response to the people's fears also met their social longings and touched the nerve center of the prevailing ecclesiastical system. The church was stripped at once of financial support and divine legitimation. The reformation of the church, whose supreme authority would no longer be the pope or canon law but rather the people of God under the Word of God, became possible. Luther's call to the German nobility—the political powers in Germany—to effect the necessary ecclesiastical and social reforms, was based on the argument that this mission was conferred on them, as "priests" through baptism and faith. The discovery of the "royal priesthood of all baptized believers" implied militant support for transformation of the church and of the political reality.

Let us now attempt a precarious leap across centuries and geography, and ask ourselves about the present meaning, in our context, of Luther's discovery. It is obvious that simply to repeat the terms of Luther's doctrine yields little. Contemporary existential concerns have

---

[3]*LW* 31:25, Thesis 1.

changed; they are couched less in terms of guilt and condemnation, and more in terms of the meaning of life and the prospects for material survival. By the same token, in the present configuration of political, social, and economic systems, the expectation of church reform is secondary. People do not long today for liberation from the church but rather from political, economic, and social systems of domination and dependency that impose ever costlier sacrifices, to the point that the cry for life is all but silenced by the structures of the power of death.

If it is true, on the one hand, that we cannot simply repeat Luther's discovery, it is also true, on the other hand, that various elements in it suggest a dynamic that is relevant even today. Justification by grace and faith implies a radical principle of equality among human beings and of the valuing of each one of them before God; it implies utter opposition to all forms of discrimination against persons and to all limitations of the quality and dignity of their lives. Persons are valued for who they are, never for what they possess, produce, or consume. Even less compatible with Luther's discovery are situations and systems based on the exploitation of a large majority of persons and peoples by a minority of persons and peoples. The degradation of any person offends God. Luther himself recognized that torture was incompatible with his discovery.

The discovery of justification by faith issues in a whole gamut of relevant meanings. Two of the most critical are

1. that what is at stake is a valuing that comes from God, which radicalizes the assertion of human value. No one is entitled to violate God's law, putting themselves in God's place; and
2. Luther's view of the church not as a hierarchical, institutional system but as a community or a people gathered together around and under the word of God. This view is vindicated by and given lively expression in the development of Christian base communities in Latin America. These communities are the instruments of the current reformation of the church.

Faith and the World

The religious and secular aspects of life existed in a confusing and contradictory relationship at the end of the Middle Ages. On the one hand, the two were clearly disassociated. To become holy—or at least relatively so—it was necessary to abandon the world, leave the mundane concerns of everyday life. The ideal of sanctity could be achieved only through monastic life; there, retreat from the world and seclusion in a convent provided adequate conditions for developing an integrated, and consequently holier, religious life. Prayer, fasting, and ascetic discipline strengthened the spirit in its communion with God. Only these people could possibly fulfill the Sermon on the Mount, whose counsels remained out of reach for ordinary believers.

Even for these ordinary believers, the practice of holiness was separated from daily life, from the world, to the degree that it was church centered: The veneration of relics, pilgrimages, and the purchase of indulgences were, at least in practice, clearer demonstrations of holy living than obeying the Ten Commandments, a regimen that also applied to ordinary Christians. Secular life was devalued, if not despised.

Alongside this profound disassociation between faith and the world, there was an equally profound identification and confusion of the two. The church had adopted a structure wholly identified with systems of secular government. Ecclesiastical positions were traded as economic and political interests dictated. The church itself was the largest feudal land owner. Worldliness and the dissolution of morals had penetrated deeply into the church, and corruption tainted even many monastic orders.

Disassociation between religious and secular aspects of life, on the one hand; identification, on the other. Luther experienced this contradictory reality in his own life. Entering the monastery of the Augustinians, known to be one of the most serious and disciplined orders, he took the road of disassociation. He discovered, nevertheless, that he had carried the secular world with him. He carried it when, despite his efforts, he had to face his limitations, his small mistakes, his doubts, and even his rebellion against an implacable, demanding God. He carried it with him especially when he realized that he lived irremediably centered in himself, as much in his many successes as in his occasional failures. Luther came to recognize that to be centered in himself, and therefore closed to God and the neighbor, was itself the ultimate nature of sin.

Recognition of this existential reality—bound up with the discovery of justification by faith—enabled Luther to look at the world more dialectically. Reality was not divided into spaces of damnation and salvation. Rather, the conflict between damnation and salvation, good and evil, justice and injustice, and faith and sin moved through all reality, as much as it constituted a battle line crossing the heart of the believer and the life of the church. For Luther, this generated a new joy in living in the world as God's creation. He considered that the beauties of nature, the taste of his favorite beer, and even a completely new appreciation of sexuality were all wonders God the creator had made available for Luther's delectation.

Family life was dignified as a realm for holiness, even if the ideal of the family that began to take shape was the precursor of the bourgeois family, in which the husband is the head and the wife is the homemaker. In a cultural context in which domestic tasks were understood as a necessary evil, and in a historical era in which women's activities outside the home were very limited, Luther's emphasis on the holiness of the family and on the activities of the homemaker redefined them as privileged expressions of service to God and to one's neighbors.

Luther also introduced a radically new understanding of occupational activity; he coined a new German word for it—*Beruf*. *Beruf* means "work" or "profession," but as its root *rufen* indicates, it also means "calling" or "vocation." Luther gave work activity a vocational cast. To have an occupation, Luther argued, was not a necessary evil nor was it to be understood essentially in terms of self-support. Above all, it was an opportunity to serve others. A new ethic, even a new discipline of work, began to emerge. The other side of this same coin was Luther's severe and frequent criticism of the mendicant orders, which Luther believed were living at the expense of others rather than working to serve others.

For Luther, then, the family, the home, and the professions were valued not in and of themselves but as opportunities for service, as spaces within which faith and love and a new kind of holiness could be actualized. Luther, having attempted to retreat from the world, returned from the monastery to the world, carrying with him the "monastic spirit" to be lived out in the world. Luther was not willing to be absorbed by the world but rather believed himself challenged to live out his faith in the world. The Christian, Luther argued, must be an instrument of faith against sin, of justice against injustice, and of love against exploitation in a battle experienced as occurring both within the Christian believer and in the surrounding world.

Luther's new vision of the world and the development of his ethic of work both reflected and interpreted a period of historical transformation. The medieval economy was giving way to the emergence of new professionals, such as artisans, business people, public officials, lawyers, and so on, and the mechanisms of production were being reordered. Although Luther's novel appreciation and ethic of work left their mark on his own and subsequent centuries, they are no longer adequate for our time for two principal reasons.

First, today we are aware that in the contemporary division of labor, many forms of work are forms of enforced service. The antagonism between labor and capital, so evident in the reordering imposed on the economies of the Third World, underscores the inadequacy of Luther's interpretation if we simply underline the vocational dimension of work. This would strengthen relations of exploitation. Second, re-pristinating Luther's work ethic under contemporary conditions risks individualizing it; the danger here is either an accommodation to or an apology for the unjust economic structures that exist today.

Luther's concepts ought rather to be augmented and applied to collective forms of action, such as participation in community associations and trade unions. In this broader sense, Luther's basic and radical notion that occupational activities are spaces for the experience of faith and holiness remains valid. There is an urgency in calling Christian people to participate fully in community activities. In Latin America, we have recognized the necessity of participating in broad, grassroots, popular movements, such as neighborhood associations, poor women's support groups, and movements of landless and homeless people. This involvement requires the same dedication and discipline Luther sought in the monastery and brought back with him to the world.

Society, Politics, and Economy

Luther lived in a period of transition from feudalism to mercantile capitalism. The feudal system was centered in fiefdoms, large tracts of land with largely self-sufficient economies. In exchange for the right to engage in subsistence farming on the feudal lord's lands, the serfs owed him a substantial portion of their labor; in exchange for the lord's protection of their lives and families, they owed him their willingness to fight in occasional wars with neighboring lords. The fiefdoms produced what was necessary for food and clothing, and their populations could count on bartering products, practically without the need for money.

The hierarchical system was legitimated by divine law represented by the church, itself a great feudal lord. Political, economic, juridical, and religious power was in the same hands or in the hands of competitors within the same class of lords.

The crusades opened the way to a new order. The development of trade began to outstrip the capacities of the barter system. Transport routes needed to be protected; they could no longer be left to the good will of the lord through whose territory goods were to be transported. Cities grew, and new artisans' professions emerged to meet the demand for new articles. More centralized political organizations became necessary. Professional armies replaced the occasional armies of the fiefdoms.

The financial resources to respond to this gamut of economic, political, and social changes came out of the coffers of the feudal lords, whose fortunes were declining, and especially of their serfs, whose rights were being curtailed at the same time as new taxes were being introduced. Some, like Luther's father, found in these rearrangements a road out of servitude into relative prosperity as small landholders or urban artisans or miners. Even so, the cost of massive structural changes was being paid by the bulk of the population.

Luther's positions on the political, economic, and social issues of his day (which are discussed in later chapters) were predicated on his insistence that there was a Christian responsibility in all these arenas. Luther would never have defended the autonomy and self-regulation of the economy, the political system, and the social order disconnected from the gospel. He did argue that the church as an institution should be free from political, economic, and social pretensions and privileges, and that Christians who held office could dedicate themselves—as "justified priests"—to tasks in the political, economic, and social arenas. Luther was persuaded that these arenas were not autonomous; on the contrary, they were subject to God's will. Everything done within them, using human reason, must be in the service of love and must take into account the needs of the people, the establishment of law, and the promotion of justice.

There is an even more important reason to identify Luther as a promoter of a new order. The feudal system was based on divine law. The church itself, which represented that law, held privilege, wealth, and power within the system it used divine authority to legitimate. Based on his most fundamental discovery—justification by faith—Luther denied that the political, economic, or social order could be divinely legitimated. The competence to legitimate came, he argued, not from divine but from human law. Therefore, legitimacy could not be grounded in a supposedly immutable divine law but must be grounded in the concrete necessities imposed by the historical process and played out materially and spiritually in the lives of real persons. These questions lay within the competence of human law and, therefore, could be dealt with by reference to that sphere.

With this concept, Luther undermined the religious legitimation of the feudal system. Within the Catholic church of that time, there was no room for this radical transformation. Denial of the church's feudal privileges and powers also meant the inevitable break with the divinely secured theological base that sustained them. Such a denial was viewed as heresy. At the same time, new economic, social, and political conditions made it impossible for the church to ignore Luther. Luther's public burning of volumes of canon law symbolized the emergence of a new order.

Let us make our last leap in time. It is important, in the first place, to register the fact that the abandonment of the political—or what is worse, complaisance in the face of injustice—cannot legitimately be ascribed to Luther. Political responsibility is implied in Christian faith. In Luther's time, the separation of the political arena from the control of the church was clearly liberating. The submission of the state to law and the understanding of law as reformable according to the real needs of the people are elements of Luther's understanding that remain valid today.

On the other hand, two words of caution are necessary. First, despite his positive contribution, Luther had a hierarchical vision of society and of politics. He issued his appeal to the princes, who were the historical subjects in the transition from feudalism to the modern era, and not to the peasants. Today, it is important to emphasize that political will is exercised from the bottom up. The people, specifically the oppressed, are the new historical subjects who seek the transformation of current situations and systems of social injustice.

Second, the pure and simple transposition of Luther's theological positions from then to now is not possible without distortion. Control of politics by the church is not a substantial risk today. On the contrary, a much more serious danger exists that we will remain subject to the will of political, economic, and social systems that claim to regulate themselves according to their own laws, impervious to criticism, to controls, and to human needs. In this modern context, the church can and must play a prophetic role vis-à-vis the state and systems that underwrite injustice and oppression.

Was Luther the representative of a new era or did he instead still belong to the medieval age that was coming to an end? He shows the marks of the transition. However, in the midst of dramatic events, wherever we look—church and spirituality; faith and world; society, politics, and economy—we see Luther making a significant, even decisive, contribution toward the new era that was emerging.

2

The Cross

Martin Luther (1483 to 1546) lived exactly at the beginning of the conquest and colonization of Latin America by the Spanish and the Portuguese. His call to reformation occurred at a time of dramatic transition. Feudalism was giving way to the first forms of mercantile capitalism. Absolute territorial states, independent of ecclesiastical or papal protection, were being formed. Renaissance culture—only sometimes religious—focused its concern on the values, beauty, and potentialities of the human being, in contrast with medieval culture, which was focused on God.

The Christological Problem in Europe and Latin America

In Luther's christology, we do not find the division between what later European research came to call the christological dogma and the historical Jesus. In Luther, they coincide. Beginning with the Enlightenment, scholars sought to reconstruct the life of Jesus on the premise that the historical Jesus, once discovered, would liberate people from the bonds forged by the church with its christological dogmas. There was a supposed contradiction between the historical Jesus and christological dogma.

Research in nineteenth-century Europe was fascinating in this respect. Many discoveries were made relative to the biblical texts, especially in the gospels; aspects of the activity and preaching of Jesus previously hidden by dogmatic theology came to light. The attempt to reconstitute a life of Jesus, however, was a failure. As Albert Schweitzer demonstrated brilliantly in his monumental *The Quest of the Historical Jesus* (1906),[1] there were as many versions of the "historical Jesus" as there were scholars, and the images varied from a socially revolutionary Jesus to a Jesus imposter and chief of a secret society, and even included a Jesus as romantic lover.

Who was the real Jesus? Martin Kähler[2] opened the way for twentieth-century European theological research to conclude that the real historical Jesus is the Christ predicated by faith. The gospel pericopes are not essentially historical reports, although they may include some historical facts; they are kerygmatic texts, proclaiming the good news of salvation in Christ. Twentieth-century theology takes up the struggle to distinguish between the historical Jesus and the proclaimed Christ. In contrast to the previous century, European theology of this century declares that it is not possible to reconstitute the life of Jesus, and that only the Christ proclaimed and received in faith matters. The apex of this modern theological evolution we find in Rudolf Bultmann for whom the story of the life of Jesus, except for the event of the cross, has no salvific relevance.

In the second half of the twentieth century, European theology is rediscovering the value of the historical Jesus not as biography but rather as the expression of the fact that the confessed Christ is precisely the one who lived and died. Faith has a concrete historical dimension. Even if we cannot reconstitute the life of Jesus, neither can we ignore such characteristics of his ministry and his proclamation as his authority over the Mosaic law and his sharing his life with the poor of the earth.

In Latin America today, on the other hand, the historical Jesus is intensely important, a situation that can be understood better in reference to Latin America's history. Throughout the history of the colonization of Latin America, two images of Jesus predominated: (1) a dead Jesus and (2) a Jesus as celestial monarch. The first image came from the Iberian peninsula, specifically from southern Spain, and reflected the experience of the common people under Arabian and Muslim domination. This Jesus suffered for the people but was defenseless, impotent, and defeated. The image of the dead Christ was carried in processions and venerated in churches. The people identified

---

[1]Albert Schweitzer, *The Quest of the Historical Jesus: A Critical Study of Its Progress from Reimarus to Wrede;* with a preface by F. C. Burkitt (New York: Macmillan, 1961).

[2]Martin Kähler, *The So-Called Historical Jesus and the Historic, Biblical Christ,* translated, edited, and with an introduction by Carl E. Braaten, foreword by Paul J. Tillich (Philadelphia: Fortress, 1964 [original: 1897]).

with the suffering of Christ and his spilled blood; they were not mo-
bilized to transform their situation of suffering.

On the other hand, Jesus as celestial monarch was the image of
the king, particularly of Spain or of Portugal. Just as the king ruled on
earth, Jesus ruled as monarch in heaven. The power, glory, and riches
of Jesus were not instruments of change but rather attributes that
legitimated the power of the Spanish or Portuguese crown.

There was another aspect to these images. The image of Jesus as
celestial monarch radically corrupted the remembrance of Christ's
sovereignty as a sovereignty over all powers—limiting and judging all
of them, in the sense of the One who "has brought down the mighty
from their thrones and lifted up the lowly" (Luke 1:52). At the same
time, during centuries of oppression, with no possible immediate escape, the image of a dead Jesus was important for the survival of the
faith and the development of critical consciousness. In the most literal
sense, it was passive resistance. The exhausted Jesus, the dead Jesus,
is the victim of evil and injustice not its legitimator.

Throughout the history of Latin America, this pair of images has
played a tragic role. The powerful Jesus, transported to heaven, underscores the effective terrestrial power of the king; a defeated Jesus
is left behind as the object of the people's identification and veneration.
The systems of domination are sustained. Can the revolutionary potential of these two images—on the one hand, of Jesus' solidarity with
those who suffer (the dead Jesus) and, on the other, Jesus' sovereignty
over all other powers (the celestial monarch)—be recuperated? Certainly, these images must be transformed if they are to express the
historical experience of liberation, through death toward new life. No
theological move that does not involve turning to the historical Jesus
is adequate to transform these traditional christological images and
their functions. In the historical Jesus, one rediscovers the active identification of Jesus with the poor, the weak, the marginalized, and the
suffering—not simply his accepting them and forgiving their sins.

Another related question remains: What is the relation between
the inspiration for the liberating activity we engage in, on the one
hand, and the liberating activity effectuated and given as a gift by
Christ, on the other? Can Luther help us with this question?

Luther's Christology

As already mentioned, Luther did not make the modern distinction
between the historical Jesus and the Christ of faith. For him, they

coincided. It was easy for him to tell the gospel stories of the life of Jesus and to translate them into his own reality, focusing on the Jesus who justifies by grace through faith. If we were to force Luther to recognize the distinction between the Christ of faith and the historical Jesus, he would choose to confess Christ's gracious work in favor of people today.

Luther preferred the gospel of John, with its long discourses of Jesus, to the synoptic gospels with their numerous accounts of events in the life of Jesus. Luther suspected and criticized what he called "historical faith," that is, faith that is satisfied with what has happened in the past and does not experience the present reality of Christ. For Luther, the historical narrative of the life of Jesus alone is not sufficient. It is merely reminiscence, not reality.

Luther's position was itself rooted in a specific historical context. He suspected that Jesus had been left in the past and that the church had taken his place. Institutional interests were superseding the proc- lamation of the gospel. Instead of being the instrument for proclaiming the actual and free salvation of Christ, the institutional church was displacing Christ, becoming administrator and commercial dispenser of Christ's grace. In protesting the traffic in indulgences, Luther was insisting on the freedom of Christ and of his gifts from the adminis- trative captivity of the institutional church. The Ninety-five Theses of 1517 reflected this perception in two fundamental themes—that "the entire life of believers . . . be one of repentance" (Thesis 1), and that "Any true Christian . . . participates in all the blessings of Christ . . . and this is granted . . . by God" (Thesis 37).[3] Luther rejected the commerce in the grace of Christ, pointing instead to the present reality of Christ and of faith in Christ.

For Luther, christology develops from redemption; christology is fundamentally soteriology. "Who and what Christ is is never a theo- retical but always a practical question."[4] Luther is not so interested in who Jesus *is* as he is in what Jesus *does* and supplies. In the work of Jesus, we discover the person of Jesus and not vice versa. In faith, we confess that all Jesus does, he does because of what he is—both God

---

[3]*LW* 31:25, 29. See also Thesis 45: "Christians are to be taught that he who sees a needy man and passes him by, yet gives his money for indulgences, does not buy papal indulgences but God's wrath." Ibid., 29.

[4]Lennart Pinomaa, *Sieg des Glaubens* (Göttingen: Vandenhoeck & Ruprecht, 1964), 90. [Translator's note: The American edition of Pinomaa's book, *Faith Vic- torious*, translated by Walter J. Kukkonen (Philadelphia: Fortress Press, 1963), leaves out the paragraph in which this statement appears in the German edition.]

and human being. But our experience and knowledge of him is provided through his works. Significantly, Luther does not emphasize the past works, the life of Jesus, but his present works, those through which he daily justifies and renews those who believe in him.

The second dimension of Luther's christology is that all that Jesus does, he does for me, for us. Traditional theological jargon speaks, in Latin, of the *pro me* or *pro nobis* of God's salvific action in Jesus. *Pro nobis* has a double meaning—in our place and in our favor. Jesus takes our place so that we can have his place. According to Luther, it is a matter of a "happy exchange" (*fröhliches Wechsel*): Jesus, the righteous one, becomes the sinner; we, the sinners, are made righteous. Humanity's sin is cast on Jesus; Jesus' righteousness is given to us. Jesus dies, we live.

"It is, of course, true that Christ is the purest of persons," Luther writes,

> but even this is not the place to stop. You do not yet have Christ, even though you know that He is God and man. You truly have Him only when you believe that this altogether pure and innocent Person has been granted to you by the Father as your High Priest and Redeemer, yes, as your Slave.[5]

The Christological Article

Luther outlines his christology in his explanation of the second article of the Apostles' Creed, the christological article. The text of the Creed itself is remarkably descriptive:

> And in Jesus Christ, his only son, our Lord: who was conceived by the Holy Spirit, born of the virgin Mary, suffered under Pontius Pilate, was crucified, died, and buried: he descended into hell, the third day he rose from the dead, he ascended into heaven, and is seated on the right hand of God, the Father almighty, whence he shall come to judge the living and the dead.

Here are the objective facts of the story of salvation in Christ. With the possible exception of the possessive *"our* (Lord)," any explicit reference to the person whose faith is being confessed is omitted. This

[5]*LW* 26:287–88.

is exactly what Luther emphasizes in his explanation. Let us look at the structure of his explanation of the second article of the Creed in the Small Catechism:

I believe that
1.   Jesus Christ, true God, begotten of the Father from eternity, and also true man,[6] born of the virgin Mary,
2.   is my Lord,
2.1 who has redeemed me, a lost and condemned creature,
2.2 delivered me and freed me from all sins, from death, and from the power of the devil,
2.3 not with silver and gold but with his holy and precious blood and with his innocent sufferings and death;
3.   in order that I may be his own,
3.1 live under him in his kingdom,
3.2 and serve him in everlasting righteousness,[7] innocence, and blessedness,
4.   even as he is risen from the dead and lives and reigns to all eternity.
This is most certainly true.[8]

If we separate the introduction ("I believe that") and the concluding affirmation ("This is most certainly true."), what remains is the content of the confession of faith in Christ. The first affirmation is the undisputed premise: "Jesus Christ, true God . . . and . . . true man." Here, Luther recapitulates the dogmatic formulation of the early church. The second affirmation—"is my Lord"—is his central thesis. Christ's lordship is the foundation of everything; "the substance of the article."[9] The implications of this thesis, characterized by the realized salvific work, follow: redemption ("has redeemed me") comes first; later, it is characterized as liberation from the oppressive powers of

---

[6]The original "Mensch" means "human being." The doctrine of incarnation affirms that God became a human being, without theological emphasis on Jesus' maleness.

[7]The original German word for "righteousness," as well as the corresponding word in Latin, Spanish, Portuguese, and other languages is equivalent to "justice"; "righteous" would correspond to "just."

[8]Small Catechism, in *The Book of Concord,* ed. Theodore G. Tappert (Philadelphia: Fortress Press, 1959), 345. Hereafter, the Small Catechism will be abbreviated SC.

[9]Large Catechism, in ibid., 413. Hereafter the Large Catechism will be abbreviated LC.

sin, death, and the power of the devil. (The Large Catechism adds the expression "all evil," powers the Large Catechism calls "tyrants and jailers."[10]) Next Luther describes the price Jesus paid: "not with silver or gold, but with his holy and precious blood and with his innocent sufferings and death."

Luther has now introduced and refers repeatedly to the person who is confessing his or her faith: "*my* Lord," "has redeemed *me*," "has delivered *me*." He has abandoned the objectivity of the Creed in order to apply it directly to whoever confesses the faith. The work of Jesus is actualized and made real today. This actuality, which is for Luther the whole point of Jesus' work, is reinforced in the third affirmation. "In order that I might be *his own*" is clearly a counterpart to "my Lord." Jesus Christ is *my* Lord, so that I may be *his*. Belonging to Jesus has immediate implications: to "live under him in his kingdom" and to serve him "in eternal righteousness, innocence, and blessedness." These are the fruits of Jesus' liberating work.

Finally, in the fourth affirmation, Luther returns to the original dogmatic premise, testifying to the victory of Christ through the resurrection—"even as he is risen from the dead and lives and reigns to all eternity"—as the foundation for the new life of the believer.

Luther's christology as he expounds it in the text of the Small Catechism hinges on these key points:

Redemption through the complete emptying of Jesus

Luther reproduces faithfully the descending line of the Apostles' Creed, so reminiscent of the famous christological hymn of Philippians 2:5–11. Jesus comes from the Father, is born of Mary, dies on the cross, descends to the world of the dead, and submits to the evil powers in order to gain the victory through the resurrection. This total emptying is the mark of the "theology of the cross," so characteristic of Luther.

Luther's explanation of the second article of the Creed reproduces this trajectory. Even when he speaks of the humanity and the life of Jesus, Luther makes a point of emphasizing Jesus' dependence. In his Christmas sermons, he refers repeatedly to Jesus' diapers; the baby Jesus, like all babies, is fragile. In his famous explication of the Magnificat, the song of Mary, Luther points out that Jesus was born to a poor and humble woman, one of the common people, someone the beautiful daughters of the rich would never have wanted even as a domestic servant.

[10]Ibid., 414.

"The more we draw Christ down into nature and into the flesh, the more consolation accrues for us,"[11] Luther says in one of his sermons. This outpouring of himself is only for our sakes; Jesus did not need to give up his glory in God. He stripped himself of glory out of compassion, Luther says. In a complete reversal of values that are dominant even today, Jesus did not buy rescue with gold or silver; rather he gave all that he could give—his own life. Here, Luther takes up the biblical theme of 1 Peter 1:18. The one who is innocent suffers in place and on behalf of those who are guilty.

The Cross as victory over tyrannical powers   Luther's christology is eminently combative. For Luther, Jesus' self-emptying is dramatized in his battle against tyrannical powers. Not only does Jesus enter into the situation of captive humanity; in a battle of historic and cosmic dimensions, he goes even into the depths of hell in order to free the imprisoned. Christ, who is eternal and insuperable righteousness, makes himself the supreme, the only sinner. All the fury and violence of the world's sin is arrayed against his righteousness. In a struggle between life and death, sin hurls itself at righteousness, damnation against blessing. According to Luther, Jesus becomes "at the same time cursed and blessed, at the same time alive and dead, at the same time grieving and rejoicing, so that He might absorb all evils in Himself and bestow all blessings from Himself."[12]

And what is the result of this awesome struggle? Christ is victorious; Satan and evil fall, defeated. The power of sin is extraordinary, but God's righteousness cannot be overcome. Death terrifies, but the life of Jesus is the "death of death." Evil is loosed over the world, but God's blessing cannot be destroyed. "Those tyrants and jailers," Luther declares,

> now have been routed, and their place has been taken by Jesus Christ, the Lord of life and righteousness and every good and blessing. He has snatched us, poor lost creatures, from the jaws of hell, won us, made us free, and restored us to the Father's favor and grace. He has taken us as his own, under his protection, in order that he may rule us by his righteousness, wisdom, power, life, and blessedness.[13]

[11]*LW* 52:12.
[12]*LW* 10:364–65.
[13]LC, op. cit., 414.

For Luther, this is the victory of the cross that transforms everything. Even in 1512, five years before the Reformation officially began, Luther said, "With Christ, everything can be overcome."[14]

New life, also marked by the experience of the Cross   The emptying of Jesus has as its counterpart a transformation in the situation of the human being, although in the opposite direction: from slavery to freedom. The Large Catechism describes it this way: Jesus is Lord and Redeemer, "that is, he who has brought us back from the devil to God, from death to life, from sin to righteousness, and now keeps us safe there."[15] In the words of the Small Catechism, "a lost and condemned creature," a captive, freed and transformed in order to serve Christ "in eternal righteousness, innocence, and blessedness."

Luther's theology has come under suspicion, often provoked by Lutherans themselves, of leading to ethical passivity. Luther's interpretation of the second article of the Apostles' Creed directly contradicts this suspicion. Here, where we might think it unnecessary for Luther to mention the ethics of the Christian, Luther addresses precisely this matter. All that Jesus does in freeing us from captivity has a clear purpose: service in righteousness, innocence, and blessedness. Luther says, "Christ is our abstraction, and we are His concretion."[16] The happy exchange that makes of Christ the righteous one, the sinner, and of us sinners, righteous ones, is an experiential, practical truth.

As long as the reality of the world and of life continue to be marked by the power of evil and of injustice, even though they are conquered in Christ, the new life of those who have been redeemed by Christ assumes the same form as his life. The provisional sign of the new life is not glory but the cross. Luther abandons the medieval figure of the imitation of Christ. It is impossible to imitate Christ, Luther maintains. But for the expression "imitation of Christ," Luther substitutes another, much more radical expression: "conformation with Christ." The term in Latin, *conformitas*, has nothing to do with conformity. It means becoming "con-formed" with Christ. Through the happy exchange between Christ and the person who believes in Christ, the believer becomes fused, or attached, to Christ and is led by Christ to a new life.

---

[14]*Christo autem praesente omnia superabilia,* in *D. Martin Luthers Werke: Kritische Gesamtausgabe.* (Weimar: Hermann Böhlaus Nachfolger, 1883–) 1, 16, 29f. Cited hereafter as *WA.*

[15]LC, op. cit., 414.

[16]*LW* 11:318.

If the expression "imitation of Christ" suggests a human capacity to repeat Christ's life, the phrase "conformation with Christ" signifies that the one who believes is placed by God on the road to new life. Free from captivity, free from sin, from death, and from the curse, this new life expresses itself in conformation with the cross of Christ, in the same descending movement of the love of God to the depths of evil and suffering, in the compassionate act of self-giving, in the disposition to carry others' loads, and in shared loneliness. Suffering, according to Luther, is the real and the royal attire of the Christian. Now and here, conformation in the cross; in the consummation, conformation in glory.[17]

Luther's Christology for Today

What does Luther's christology offer us in the context of current Latin American reality, and perhaps even outside that context?

The historical Jesus We will not find in Luther any formal support for our rediscovery of the value of the historical Jesus for the practice of liberation. This is the case principally because for him the distinction between the historical Jesus and the Christ of faith had not yet emerged. We might even find what we could call "spiritualizing tendencies" in Luther's criticism of "historical faith." There is, however, a specific historical context for Luther's rediscovery of the freedom and grace of God in the face of the church's commercialized usurpation of the means of grace. In new historical situations in which the church does not function as a structure of domination but rather as an instrument of liberation, Luther's assertions cannot simply be repeated without modification.

One good example would be the issue of the paradigmatic marks of Jesus, which in Luther is related to the issue of the hidden God.

---

[17]Of course, this idea can be and has been all too often abused, when exploitative, dominant, and oppressive forces suggest to exploited, dominated, and oppressed people that they must endure suffering with patience: masters over against slaves, whites over against blacks and native peoples, men over against women. With Leonardo Boff we must distinguish between a suffering that is imposed on people—and to which the only possible response for a Christian is to protest and resist—and a suffering that is a consequence of solidarity, a "suffering that is born in the struggle against suffering." (Leonardo Boff, *Passion of Christ, Passion of the World* [Maryknoll, N.Y.: Orbis Books, 1987], 117.)

Jesus was born in a stable, not even a house. And he will die on a cross, between two murderers, outside the city, in a profaned and condemned place. The life of Jesus unfolds between these two moments, the one of birth and the one of death, both in weakness. The trajectory of his life is in conformity with this principle and with this end. In light of faith, of our trust, we see God present there. Without faith, it would not be possible to see God's presence; we would have to see Jesus as a failure.

The trademark one sees in the course of Jesus' life is his presence in solidarity at the side of all those who are in need, who are marginalized, and who suffer because of injustice and oppression. This begins with the sick, with those who suffer physical needs, and because of this, perhaps are socially marginalized. He is there with them. It proceeds with women, whose dignity Jesus asserts through his words and, above all, through his deeds. It continues with those who have been dispossessed from the land, with the hungry, and with those pursued by evil spirits. He blesses the poor, who in the gospel of Luke are not the poor in spirit but the physically poor, those impoverished by a system that generates poor people.

These are the trademarks of Jesus, and today one cannot simply spiritualize them to make a Platonic Christ, ideal and harmonious for everyone. In these marks of his life, we ought to seek the meaning of the historical Jesus.

A Christology in soteriological perspective   It is important to understand christology from the standpoint of soteriology so that it is not corrupted into a legitimating ideology, as it has been in the image of Christ as celestial monarch. If Christ's work is the entry point for the person of Christ, then the image of king—of celestial monarch— must be measured by that which this particular king, Christ, does. The sovereignty of Christ is performative, following the path of self-emptying, the path of the cross. Our rediscovery of the value of the historical Jesus, in particular his active identification with the poor and the oppressed, ought to be integrated into the theology of the cross and of the kenosis of Jesus.

A word about Christ's resurrection might be appropriate at this point. It cannot be disassociated from the cross; rather, the resurrection is given in the midst of the experience of the cross. To find hope within a hopeless situation, to have hope, is an experience of resurrection in the midst of a reality of the cross. The resurrection happens always in the midst of situations of evil, of alienation, of the cross. At times of darkness, of the most violent repression, hope, mobilization, and the possibility of escape are born; such moments are concrete, palpable, historical manifestations of an experience of resurrection.

This applies not only in social but also in personal experience. A person who is suffering, perhaps from some illness, is given the strength, the energy, to live with the confidence that the resurrection of Jesus Christ is coming, even though it does not look that way from the objective configuration of the situation.

Perhaps an example from Brazil is appropriate. In the midst of terrible violence and a terrifying economic crisis that has been imposed on the Brazilian people, on the peoples of the Third World in general, by the financial interests of the great powers, international bankers— in the midst of this situation the strength is given to mobilize, to gather together in solidarity. This surely constitutes a sign of new life and as such, of the resurrection of Christ.

A combative Christology   Luther's christology is dynamic and combative, never static and accommodated. This is especially clear when his theology concentrates on the cross, the point of confluence in the historical and cosmic battle between evil and righteousness, curse and blessing, and death and life. Here, there is no defeated resignation but rather shared and redemptive suffering. The dead Jesus of popular Latin American veneration may be the expression of re- signed and impotent suffering (and may also be an image that helps people survive under oppression), but Christ crucified, as interpreted by Luther, is divine love's combatant. His cross is not defeat, but rather the victorious culmination of an all-out battle. Hence *Christus victor*— victorious Christ.

Conformation with the Cross of Christ   The suspicion that accenting the activity of God might paralyze human activity is incon- sistent with all that Luther discovered and proclaimed. The more concentration there is on the redeeming activity of God, the greater the liberating activity of those who believe in Christ. We are free from the necessity to imitate Christ because his work is fundamental, un- repeatable, and complete. But for the same reason we are free for new liberating actions, in conformation with the cross of Christ and in accordance with what our imagination and discernment show us to be works of love.

Lutheran churches over the course of history have lost the com- bative aspect present in Luther's christology as well as the concept of conformation with the cross of Christ. Lutheran churches established themselves under the tutelage of political powers. And so a situation was created opposite from the one Luther had struggled with. Luther struggled against the political hegemony of the institutional Catholic church of his day. He fought the papal claim to exercise power also over the political.

Luther specifies and gives great value to the political task, and assigns it, in a historical perception that was perhaps correct at that moment, to the princes. But very soon, the territorial churches were organized and linked to the princes. There were disturbances, confrontations, war, and division between the Protestant church and the Catholic church until an agreement was reached. The principle that emerged was *cuius regio eius religio*, according to which the religious fidelity of persons depended on the religious option of the prince who exercised power in that territory. The possibility existed that if one was not in agreement with the prince's choice, one could go to some neighboring territory where the prince had made another religious choice. But often this was not feasible, and one had to submit to the prince's choice. In this way, the territorial churches were created. With the development of political absolutism, the churches were domesticated and integrated into the state political systems. This element contributed greatly to the fact that Lutheran churches were often conservative.

Throughout the course of the history of the Lutheran church, the combative aspect has been forgotten along with the necessity of following Jesus Christ in his path, of joining Jesus Christ in his kenosis, his emptying out. Therefore, it is vital to perceive and discover anew: Linked together with Christ by his redeeming work, we are his liberating partners in the experience of the cross and in the struggle against evil today.

3

Conversion, Liberation, and Justification

In his novel *Aunt Julia and the Scriptwriter,* the Peruvian writer Mario Vargas Llosa describes Gumercindo Tello. He was not a criminal type, Vargas writes, but something "in a certain sense much, much more serious"—a believer. Gumercindo Tello, a Jehovah's Witness, is accused of having forced himself on a girl of thirteen. In him, Vargas writes, one could detect

> that serenely stubborn gaze of a man who knows, who has no doubts, who has solved all his problems. Rather short in stature, he was a young man, doubtless not yet thirty, whose frail physique, nothing but skin and bones, proclaimed to the four winds his scorn for bodily nourishment and the material world, with hair cropped so short his skull was nearly bare, and a swarthy complexion. He was dressed in a gray suit the color of ashes, the costume neither of a dandy nor of a beggar but something in between, which was dry now but very wrinkled from the baptismal rites, a white shirt, and ankle boots with cleats. Just one glance sufficed for the judge—a man with a flair for anthropology—to discern immediately his distinctive personality traits: circumspection, moderation, fixed ideas, imperturbability, a spiritual vocation.[1]

Here are the marks of the religious fanatic: determination to live an excessively regimented religious life, a sense of missionary zeal, and a break with social reality. If we were able to factor out these fanatical traits, we could not help noticing one essential element of all Christian faith that is lived with integrity: a refusal to accommodate

[1] Mario Vargas Llosa, *Aunt Julia and the Scriptwriter,* translated by Helen R. Lane (New York: Farrar, Straus and Giroux, Inc., 1982), 115.

itself to situations of perversion and alienation in human relationships and in society.

Conversion

Seventeenth-century Protestant orthodoxy was a great intellectual accomplishment that sought with logical rigor and extreme zeal to establish the objectivity of faith, reproducing the divine revelation in faithful formulas. What was required of the believer was to assent to the doctrinal truth or truths that orthodoxy had established. To believe was to commit the intellect to the formulated doctrines.

Pietism, bringing historical criticism to bear on orthodoxy, protested its sterile and rigid concept of faith. Later, it is true, pietism incorporated many of the elements orthodoxy had elaborated—for example, its literalism in the interpretation of Scripture. But pietism abandoned the rigid objectivity of orthodoxy, emphasizing instead the personal appropriation of the faith. What mattered was not the assent of the intellect, but the surrender of the heart. One did not ask, What is the truth to which I must adhere? but rather, What does the Word of God say "to me"? The orthodox were convinced that the objective truth configured the life of those who, through faith, adhered to it; for pietists, on the other hand, the living of the faith—or better yet, new life—was the key.

If orthodoxy fell prey to distanced objectivity, pietism was tempted to arbitrary subjectivity. In pietism, personal surrender and the action of God, the person and God, meet in the experience of conversion. The emphasis pietism places on the necessity of a personal conversion is clearly a call for authenticity and radical renewal. The converted person surrenders the "old I" to a God who makes demands and at the same time forgives. Together with a radical judgment of the past, radical possibilities are opened for the future. Conversion separates "before" from "after." "Before" is characterized as bad and empty, whereas the "new" is replete with meaning and wonder.

Even today, the pietist movement is fueled by its perception of the need for conversion all human beings have, the effective experience of conversion or new birth, and the constant call for the conversion of others. Pietists see signs of spiritual decadence when these elements are ignored.

The theology of liberation understands the term "conversion" in a different way—as conversion "to the Realm of God and to the neighbor." Hugo Assmann writes of "conversion to the Realm of God as conversion to the transformation within history, and conversion to God within conversion to human being."[2] Gustavo Gutiérrez, for his part, approaches "conversion to the neighbor" in these terms: "To know God is to do justice" and "Christ in the neighbor."[3] This interpretation of conversion comprises at least two characteristic traits. First, love of God and love of the neighbor are fused. Assmann writes about "the Christian paradox of the radical unity of the love of God and the love of the neighbor."[4] Second, conversion is historicized. Again, Assmann: "This is the Christian paradox that has tremendous revolutionary meaning: in order to be converted to God and the prospect of God's Realm, it is necessary to be converted, here and now, to humanity and humanity's history." He concludes, "It is in the struggle for human liberation that the love of God materializes (see Matthew 25)."[5] Gutiérrez also invokes this dimension in his chapter entitled "Encountering God in History," which concludes with a section entitled, significantly, "A Spirituality of Liberation."[6]

Compared with pietism, liberation theology's understanding of conversion is broader, given its historical and material character, and has a different focus, which is defined by the concept of liberation. Although pietism places its emphasis on new life and personal decision, it also interprets conversion as bound up with God and issuing from God, by means of God's Spirit. New life and love for the neighbor follow it—logically, and perhaps also chronologically. The activity of God in the person is understood as an indispensable first premise—as that without which all the rest is vain, wrong, fleeting, and without divine blessing.

For the theology of liberation, the pietist perspective is too narrow, tending toward individualism and away from historical concreteness. Liberation theologians believe that the term "liberation" does greater

---

[2]Hugo Assmann, *Teología desde la praxis de la liberación* (Salamanca: Sígueme, 1973), 147f. [Translator's note: This portion of Assmann's book was not translated for the American version, *Theology for a Nomad Church* [Maryknoll, N.Y.: Orbis Books, 1976]. Quotations cited here were translated by the translator.]

[3]Gustavo Gutiérrez, *A Theology of Liberation,* translated and edited by Sister Caridad Inda and John Eagleson (Maryknoll, N.Y.: Orbis Books, 1973), 194, 196.

[4]Assmann, *Teleogia desde la praxis de la liberación,* 148.

[5]Ibid., 148.

[6]Gutiérrez, *A Theology of Liberation,* 189, 203.

justice to the integrity of the human being as a social and historical being, encouraging the transformation of history and the establishment of a more humane and communal life and society.

For Luther, the key term is "justification," not conversion or liberation. Is justification a self-respecting partner in a dialogue with the other two, or is it expendable, obsolete, or illegitimate?

Justification

For many years, Luther resisted the idea of publishing an anthology of his works. At last, in 1545, near the end of his life, he acceded and wrote a preface—the *Preface to the Complete Edition of Luther's Latin Writings*[7]—in which he reflected on the early days of the Reformation, almost three decades before. As Luther describes his discovery, or rediscovery, of justification, it becomes clear that justification by faith, as a doctrine, expressed for him a profound personal experience.

First as a monk and later as a professor of biblical theology, Luther had struggled with the question, "How can I find a merciful God?" Late medieval theology offered the assurance that "to the one who does everything one possibly can" (*facere quod in se est*), God gives grace. God was righteous and punished sin but was also disposed to offer grace on the condition that one did "all one possibly could." Grace came from God. But the person should make an effort to merit, to deserve, grace—even "just" to the extent possible.

Luther went to great lengths to do whatever he possibly could. Monastic piety and theology recommended constant prayer, rigid exercises of ascetic devotion, minute self-examination, sincere penitence, and a disposition to do the most humble tasks. All this Luther practiced to perfection, it would seem.

Despite all his efforts, however, Luther believed he moved from one failure to another. Von Staupitz, his superior, counseled him to concentrate on the cross of Christ rather than on himself, and this advice helped. Still, Luther could not let go of his obsessive and scrupulous self-examination. How could he? If he ignored even his smallest offenses, how could he have done everything within his power to merit God's grace? And if he did not do everything within his power,

[7]*LW* 34:327–38.

how could he attain grace? because that was the condition for God's gracious gift. The demand to do "just" what was within his reach, apparently a reasonable request, imposed an unbearable burden. Luther dissolved into desperation.

He began to believe himself condemned without appeal and to hate God. His God, reputed to be generous and disposed to give grace to those who "just" did what they could, seemed increasingly tyrannical. Luther's hatred toward God grew even more in light of Paul's statement in Romans 1:17a that "In it the righteousness of God is revealed":

> ". . . as if, indeed, it is not enough that miserable sinners, eternally lost through original sin, are crushed by every kind of calamity by the law of the decalogue, without having God add pain to pain by the gospel and also by the gospel threatening us with his righteousness and wrath!" Thus I raged with a fierce and troubled conscience. Nevertheless, I beat importunately upon Paul at that place, most ardently desiring to know what St. Paul wanted.
>
> At last, by the mercy of God, meditating day and night, I gave heed to the context of the words, namely, "In it the righteousness of God is revealed, as it is written, 'He who through faith is righteous shall live.' " There I began to understand that the righteousness of God is that by which the righteous lives by a gift of God, namely by faith. And this is the meaning: the righteousness of God is revealed by the gospel, namely, the passive righteousness with which merciful God justifies us by faith, as it is written, "He who through faith is righteous shall live."[8]

Luther's search for a merciful God received an unexpected response. In the midst of the battle of doubts and hatred toward God, in the confrontation with the biblical text, a radical change occurred that Luther recorded in the following words: "Here I felt that I was altogether born again and had entered paradise itself through open gates."[9]

Luther's account, which was written thirty years after the event, retained the indelible mark of his personal experience. Pietists could hardly avoid seeing here an account of authentic conversion: confrontation with the biblical text, struggle and resistance, personal surrender—and entrance, now freed, into paradise. The desperation of one condemned cedes place to the happy security of one justified. A

[8]Ibid., 337.
[9]Ibid.

change in Luther's understanding of God—from One who is terrible in fury to One who saves in mercy—accompanies the change from hostility toward God to happiness in God. Sections of Luther's "table talk," especially from the years 1532, 1538, and 1540, add to the evidence of the decisiveness of this event in Luther's life.[10]

Luther expressed this experience, too, in the hymns he composed, the most important one of which is "Nun freut euch, lieben Christen gemein" (Dear Christians, let us now rejoice).[11] The melody is a joyful popular tune adapted by Luther. The first stanza expresses the justified person's happiness:

> Dear Christians, let us now rejoice,
> And dance in joyous measure:
> That of good cheer and with one voice,
> We sing in love and pleasure.
> Of what to us our God hath shown,
> And the sweet wonder he hath done;
> Full dearly hath he wrought it.

The next two stanzas look back at what preceded justification, describing the captivity and the desperation of those who feel condemned:

> Forlorn and lost in death I lay,
> A captive to the devil,
> My sin lay heavy, night and day,
> For I was born in evil.
> I fell but deeper for my strife,
> There was no good in all my life,
> For sin had all possessed me.

[10]*LW* 54:193–94 (Table Talk no. 3232c); 308–9 (no. 4007); *WA* TR 5, 26, 18–26 (no. 5247). The important no. 5247 is not in *LW;* the one with that number should be numbered no. 5252, according to the original in *WA.*

[11]*LW* 53:219–20. The hymn appears in English in the *Lutheran Book of Worship* (Minneapolis: Augsburg Publishing House and Philadelphia: Board of Publication, Lutheran Church in America, 1978), as #299, "Dear Christians, Let Us Now Rejoice." Unfortunately, this translation has consistently spiritualized and weakened Luther's original text. For example, in stanza 5, the pointed challenge of the original "salvation for the *poor*" was blunted by the universalized "bring to *all* salvation"; in stanza 6, "my *poor* form" was sentimentalized into "a *servant's* form"; in stanza 7, "I will *fight* thy *battle*" was descandalized into "for you I *strive* and *wrestle*"; stanza 10 narrows "the kingdom's work" to the realm of our "*preaching*," while in the original it comprises our "*doing* and preaching" (italics added by author).

My good works they were worthless quite,
A mock was all my merit;
My will hated God's judging light,
To all good dead and buried.
E'en to despair me anguish bore,
That nought but death lay me before;
To hell I fast was sinking.

Stanzas four to ten move from describing Luther's personal experience to an account of the history of salvation. Before looking at them, however, it is worth pointing out some significant aspects of Luther's understanding of justification that also allow us to discern important differences between it and the pietist understanding of conversion.

Although Luther never stopped proclaiming justification by faith in his writings and in innumerable sermons, he was very sparing—especially in his sermons—in describing his personal experience. He did not use his own experience of justification to persuade others to attempt to have the same experience. In fact, this would have represented the denial of justification by grace. Significantly, at the end of his life, Luther could no longer identify the precise date of his "discovery" of justification. In his *Preface to the Latin Writings*, he placed it in 1519, although it almost certainly occurred several years before.

Luther distinguished between the subjective and the objective dimensions of justification. The personal experience, as we see, is necessary and profound, but it is also particular and nontransferable. Luther's testimony is never "personal"; for Luther, this is clearly not what is important. What is important is the objective reality of justification in Christ.

As mentioned earlier, on the altar of the church in the city of Wittenberg there is a painting by Lucas Cranach the Elder showing Luther in the pulpit, preaching to the gathered community. In the center of the painting is Christ on the cross, toward whom Luther points with his finger and his arm outstretched, directing the attention of the community. In the cross, his gesture says, there is justification. The community can receive there its good news, in joyful and liberating faith. Each person, in his or her own way, will have a personal experience, but no personal experience as such can or should take the place of the work of Christ.

Luther's hymn continues from the fourth stanza, not with Luther's personal experience but with the history of salvation, a narrative of the salvific work of Christ:

> Then God was sorry on his throne
> To see such torment rend me;
> His tender mercy he thought on,
> His good help he would send me.
> He turned to me his father-heart;
> Ah! then was his no easy part,
> For of his best it cost him.

In the following stanzas we can see the characteristic features of Luther's christology appear—the descending, kenotic line; Jesus' solidarity and struggle; the reciprocity between Jesus and the believer; new life:

> To his dear Son he said: "Go down,
> 'Tis time to take compassion.
> Go down, my heart's exalted crown,
> Be the poor man's salvation.
> Lift him from out sin's scorn and scath,
> Strangle for him that cruel Death,
> That he with thee live ever."

> The Son he heard obediently,
> And by a maiden mother,
> Pure, tender—down he came to me,
> For he would be my brother.
> Secret he bore his strength enorm,
> He went about in my poor form,
> For he would catch the devil.

> He said to me: "Hold thou by me,
> Thy matters I will settle;
> I give myself all up for thee,
> And I will fight thy battle.
> For I am thine, and thou art mine,
> And my place also shall be thine;
> The enemy shall not part us."

The eighth stanza describes the price paid to free those who were condemned:

"He will as water shed my blood,
My life he from me reave will;
All this I suffer for thy good—
To that with firm faith cleave well.
My life from death the day shall win,
My innocence shall bear thy sin,
So art thou blest forever."

The ninth stanza notes the protection that issues from the risen and exalted Jesus for the believer who lives the way of the cross:

"To heaven unto my Father high,
From this life I am going;
But there thy Master still am I,
My spirit on thee bestowing,
Whose comfort shall they trouble quell,
Who thee shall teach to know me well,
And in the truth shall guide thee."

Finally, the tenth stanza calls ardently to faith and discipleship:

"What I have done, and what I've said,
Shall be thy doing, teaching,
So that God's kingdom may be spread—
All to his glory reaching.
Beware what men would bid thee do,
For that corrupts the treasure true;
With this last word I leave thee."

For Luther the discovery, or rediscovery, of justification always maintained its central, decisive, and liberating character. But Luther was a volatile person who experienced many radical and abrupt changes throughout his life. His entry into the monastery in 1505, for example, was a precipitous decision made as he struggled against his fear of death in the middle of a storm. In saying farewell to his friends and companions in law school, he declared decisively: "Today you see me once more; hereafter never again!" His friends could not dissuade him from his resolution to abandon a promising career in law in order to enter the monastery.

Throughout his life, Luther was frequently distressed. Fears, doubts, weaknesses, and anxieties assailed him. Nevertheless, he always found strength to go on, not in the memory of his personal experience of justification but in the assurance of the work consummated by Christ for him.

In a certain sense, Luther was adept in what we would call "permanent conversion." Once again the first of his Ninety-five Theses is important: Jesus Christ ". . . willed the entire life of believers to be one of repentance."[12] In the catechisms, he interpreted the significance of baptism, which is effectuated only once: ". . . the old Adam in us, together with all sins and evil lusts, should be drowned by *daily* sorrow and repentance and be put to death, and that the new man[13] should come forth *daily* and rise up, cleansed and righteous, to live forever in God's presence."[14] Because of this, each person ought to consider baptism ". . . as the daily garment which he is to wear all the time. Every day he should be found in faith and amid its fruits, every day he should be suppressing the old man and growing up in the new."[15] The experience of justification, once given, does not eliminate the need to experience it daily; on the contrary, it should open the way for this daily experience. Luther emphasized not the conversion that has occurred but rather the conversion that continues to happen.

Luther described the life of the believer as that of someone who is simultaneously righteous and sinful. However, he refused to point to his own experience as an example because, he believed, that would be the clearest expression of perseverance in sin, through arrogance and vanity, and of legalism, precisely that from which he had been freed by grace through faith. Instead, he pointed repeatedly to the grace and righteousness of God. One of Luther's prayers is illuminating: "Dear Lord and Savior, help us remain pious sinners and not become blasphemous saints!"[16]

Not his own experience, but the reality of justification, rooted in the merciful work of God, was what was important to Luther. The doctrine of justification became essential for him. "Nothing in this article can be given up or compromised."[17]

---

[12]*LW* 31:25.
[13]Original: "human being."
[14]SC, ibid., 349, emphasis added.
[15]LC, ibid., 449.
[16]Quoted in Hans Mayer, *Martin Luther: Leben und Glaube* (Gütersloh: Gütersloher Verlagshaus Mohn, 1982), 265. [Translated by translator.]
[17]The Smalcald Articles, in the *Book of Concord,* op. cit., 292.

Justification as Liberation

In response to the suspicion that Luther's doctrine of justification could lead to ethical disinterest or paralysis, several points are worth emphasizing:

First, in shifting his attention from the subjective to the objective dimension of justification, Luther placed the justified person in the larger context of the salvific history of God in Christ. This is christology's significance for justification. The story of Jesus, poor and rejected but still in our favor, immediately broadens the forms of Christ's works beyond the merely individualistic.

Second, the liberation represented by Luther's discovery, or rediscovery, of justification through grace and faith had a historical dimension as well. The response Luther found to his own personal problem was also liberating for a whole generation. His discovery undermined an ecclesiastical system that was imposing on the people multiple burdens of conscience and financial tribute, of which the sale of indulgences was only one. Insofar as Luther was also voicing the complaints of the German nation against internal and external ecclesiastical exploitation, his discovery helped fortify national secular political power against "foreign" domination by Rome.

Third, the notion that justification would carry with it an ethical passivity simply does not correspond to what we can verify in Luther's life and teaching. For Luther, passivity occurred exclusively in the relationship with God. When Luther was freed, he was freed from "doing all he could." Justification by faith is never all there is. It immediately reveals the importance of commitment to one's neighbors and to their needs. Luther's treatise on *The Freedom of a Christian* (1520) deals with precisely these two phrases of what is essentially a single melody: (1) the believer's marvelous freedom in relation to God in faith and (2) the radical commitment to the neighbor in love.[18] Many of his other writings, among them the *Treatise on Good Works* and other treatises related to social, economic, and political issues, deal with the inescapable ethical commitment of the Christian. It is precisely the Christian's freedom before God, Luther insists, that permits ethical concerns to be focused on the neighbor's needs instead of being a cover for one's own benefit.

[18]*LW* 31:333–77.

At this point, it seems appropriate to expand on the question whether Luther's emphasis on passivity in justification would also lead to ethical passivity and, therefore, to the denial of the task of liberation. Let us remind ourselves that the task of liberation emerges as a response to the analysis we make of social reality. In general terms, it is a task of Christian love. According to Leonardo Boff,[19] there are two ways to approach the problem. The first is sacramental; here, in a very Catholic, Franciscan sense, that is, by means of direct contact with need. One sees a poor person, one has compassion on that person and thinks, "I must do something!" and one gives the person alms. One attempts to help in an immediate way but not reflectively, without asking whether or not this really helps the poor person.

The second approach is scientific-analytic; here, one seeks to identify the causes of poverty. And one discovers that there are no poor, but only *impoverished*. A method for attacking the causes of injustice and oppression in an organized way also becomes necessary. This is by no means beyond the theological possibilities present in Luther's theology. Luther certainly did not develop in his day the Latin American theology of today. But he does say that the political task is a task for Christians, that one must reflect with reason freed by faith in order that it become an instrument of love, that one must reflect on the effectiveness of a given action.

Therefore, we seek those paths that establish justice and community. This has nothing to do with passivity as Luther experienced it in justification by faith. Reflecting on what we ought to do, having had that experience, Luther says in his controversy with the antinomians that it is necessary to develop new "decalogues." These certainly arise out of a particular analytical awareness of the given situation. Yet, when we emphasize the passivity in justification we may—without wanting to, perhaps—be justifying a comfortable ethic. The passivity of Luther's experience of justification is used to justify not participating in the task of liberation.

We can hardly accuse Luther himself of being passive. He did act in error—for example, in the matter of the peasants—but it would be difficult to describe Luther at any moment in his life as tranquil, passive, or indifferent. Sometimes, in fact, he was too precipitate. Perhaps he should have had to think a little more before acting and speaking.

[19]Leonardo Boff and Clodovis Boff, *Salvation and Liberation*, translated by Robert R. Barr (Maryknoll, N.Y.: Orbis Books, 1984), 2–3.

Part of the problem is rooted in the distinction Luther makes between the political and social task—a task that, although necessary, is provisional and terrestrial—and justification, in which he emphasizes the action of God. In Luther's time, the distinction between these two realms opened very broad possibilities for activity in the political terrain.

Perhaps this helps us understand, although it does not justify, Luther's position in relation to the peasants. Luther feared that a terrestrial proposal would be legitimated religiously. Therefore, he rejected the attempt of the peasants to use the Bible to legitimate their political and social demands. He was afraid that the hard won victory over religious control of political power would be reversed, and that with this the gospel, distorted into law, would be lost. On this point, Luther has an almost apocalyptic vision, according to which we are in the decisive and final years. These are the reasons for his actions and pronouncements, even if they are not justifiable.

Today, our emphasis must be different. It is important that life under grace, a life of compassion, not be understood as an individualistic life, a mere inner peace, but rather a communitary, collective life that takes concrete form in our societies. The experiences of the Christian base communities, in sharing their life, are concrete manifestations of an ecclesial realization in which mercy becomes palpable through solidarity, through living and struggling together. It goes beyond the dimension of self-satisfaction. We should perhaps be more cautious in relation to the emphasis on passivity, which could be misleading, and see that the realm of God must become visible by means of signs that are made visible by those who follow Jesus Christ.

Life under grace is always life threatened, because it is never realized totally. It is in a permanent tension, the tension between cross and resurrection. Luther's observation is correct, that the realm of God is *of God*; it is not the realm we make. We are in a provisional mode, still heading toward the consummation of God's realm. This recognition ought to be complemented by another one—namely, that partial, provisional realizations of the realm of God in our reality, even if they are only provisional, are necessary.

Conversion, Liberation, and Justification

Let us return to the problem with which we began this chapter, and observe whether or not we can now draw some provisional conclusions based on our reflections on Luther's doctrine of justification.

Conversion and justification   To underestimate or overlook the pietist emphasis on the need for conversion and on this conversion as the work of God through the Holy Spirit would be to renounce fundamental biblical elements. However, the call to conversion is perverted when, using the need for conversion as a point of departure, a law is laid down for the only acceptable type of conversion. Luther's distinctions between the subjective and objective aspects of the salvific event, as well as his perspective on daily conversion, are helpful here.

The relation between baptism and conversion is also relevant. It is perhaps even clearer today than it was in Luther's time that baptism, especially infant baptism, is no substitute for conversion. Nor can conversion take the place of baptism, unless we are seeking to substitute human experience for divine action. Recall the connection Luther made between baptism, effectuated once, and daily conversion. The value of understanding conversion as a daily process diminishes if it is thought of as a work unconnected with baptism and the action of God. Pietism rightly reminds us of the free action of God in conversion; God's freedom does not hinge on the immediate "ethicization" of conversion. At the same time, it would also be an abuse of God if we allowed ourselves to separate the turn to God in justification from the turn to our neighbor in love. Conversion is not simply a personal change; it also reflects, in good measure, historical transitions. In Latin American Protestantism, conversions reflected the transition of a traditional, postcolonial society into the liberal world; this is where the value attributed to subjectivity entered in, exercising a positive and significant role. In periods of historical transition, the experience of conversion necessarily takes different forms, and the characteristic features that represent the change from the old to the new ought not to be discarded. And today, individualistic subjectivity must be superseded by an awareness of collective social realities and the discovery of the poor and marginated as decisive historical protagonists.

Liberation and justification   The saving event that occurred in Jesus Christ and that has Jesus Christ as its point of departure is not always adequately expressed by the same term. What is important is not the dogmatic formulation in itself but rather the reality that the formulation manages to express.

Even in the New Testament, the saving event comes to expression in a variety of terminological and doctrinal forms. The synoptic gospels emphasize the proximity of the realm of God. John describes the revelation of the glory of Jesus. Paul can talk about both justification (for the Jews in Rome, for example) and reconciliation (for the Christians in Corinth).

In Luther's time, the juridical terminology of justification became important; the problem of guilt and condemnation worried not only Luther but a whole people and a whole era. But we would be deceiving ourselves if we thought that the doctrine of justification, as Luther formulated it, could retain the same relevance for all eras and situations. Such a perennial theology does not exist.

In *The Courage to Be*, Paul Tillich contends that the doctrine of "justification" responded particularly well to the anxieties and needs of Luther's time, the death throes of the Middle Ages in the transition to the modern age. For the problems of our time, which Tillich characterizes as emptiness and meaninglessness, he suggests the term "acceptance" as a more appropriate response. Of course, this approach reflects the context of an opulent society. In Latin America, a context of domination and dependence, the term "liberation" is particularly well suited to express the "wholeness" of salvation and its character as a process as well as its personal and its historical dimensions. "Liberation" also communicates the biblical dialectic of being free from (a slavery) and free for (a service), weaving God's gratuitous action together with our human ethical commitment.

In the Latin American context and situation, however, the doctrine of justification has at least two liberating roles to play. First, it can function as a critical principle with respect to the institutional church when the church interposes itself between God's liberating activity and human activity for liberation. When this happens, human activity becomes the response to demands imposed by the institutional church and stops being a liberating process in the midst of the concrete needs of marginalized and exploited people. Justification by faith (and only by faith) unmasks the ecclesiastical demands with which the church stops being an instrument of salvation and transforms itself into another system of domination.

Second, it is not difficult to trace a route from justification by grace (and only by grace) toward the inalienable value of every human being. The ideology of human rights did not emerge directly from the Christian faith, much less from Protestantism, but rather from humanist rationalism. But justification by grace radicalizes respect for human dignity, in that it attributes this dignity to the free will of God and not to nature. Over against the multiplicity of ideological and social claims such as production and property, culture and power, the valuing of the human being for what he or she *is*, even and especially in deficiency, weakness, impotence, and marginality, returns us to the path that leads to Jesus of Nazareth, born in a stable and killed on a cross.

4

Scripture

The Bible and the Latin American Churches

Significant questions are being asked these days about Bible reading in Latin American churches. Among them: Is the Bible being forgotten by Protestants while it becomes the book of Catholics? Are Protestants getting tired of using the Bible while Catholics are increasingly excited about it? Is the Protestant reading of the Bible increasingly stale and repetitive while the Catholic reading generates creativity and renewal?

The relation of the Latin American Catholic church to the Bible has changed dramatically. Before the Second Vatican Council (1962 to 1965), the Bible was conspicuous by its virtual absence in Catholic practice. It was reserved, if it was used at all, for priests and theologians. When it was used, the emphasis was not biblical but dogmatic. The doctrine of the church absorbed and neutralized the biblical testimony. The faithful were to learn the practice of piety and other basics of the catechism but very little of biblical history.

No doubt this situation was very much tied to the spirit of the Counter-Reformation and the post-Tridentine period, which was disposed to reject anything Protestant. Because the Reformation had raised the flag of *sola scriptura*, it was important—or so it seemed—to lift up the interpretive and doctrinal authority of the (Roman Catholic) church. This tendency culminated in Vatican I (1870), which established papal infallibility in matters of faith and morals when the pope speaks *ex cathedra*.

The Catholic church, although it never defined itself as being above Scripture, judged it necessary to guarantee the unity and legitimacy of its interpretation by establishing an authoritative interpretive body.

43

Given a correct, authoritative, and unquestionable interpretation, why distribute the Bible, which was in any case difficult to understand and invariably distorted by the Protestants? Besides, Roman theology had come to speak of two parallel sources of divine revelation: Scripture and tradition. According to this view, not only was there one legitimate and authoritative interpretation of Scripture, but also the revelation and the truths transmitted by the tradition had been "attached" to those of Scripture. The magisterium saw to their legitimate and authoritative transmission.

The profound renewal that began in the Catholic church with Vatican II was due in good measure to the rediscovery of the Bible that had begun during the decades before the council. Vatican II made official a new approach to the Bible and opened the way for a new use of Scripture. For example, Vatican II explicitly rejected the theory of two sources of revelation, placing the tradition parallel with Scripture. Rather, according to the Council, the apostolic tradition prior to the recording of Scripture flowed in a written form into the Scriptural tradition; the ecclesiastical tradition after the recording of Scripture was and is the interpretation and development of it. That development is the realization of the normative dimension of Scripture, as the written body of the apostolic tradition. Although the authority of the magisterium remains for the interpretation and discernment of the dogmatic development of Scripture, it does not have at its disposal an additional, independent source of revelation.

Vatican II also encouraged renewed exegetical research in the Bible, acknowledging in this way that the interpretations given by the magisterium, despite their authenticity, did not exhaust the wealth of Scripture. That resource ought continuously to be mined. Against literalism, the validity of modern historical-critical methods for biblical exegesis was recognized. This development brought the significant currents in Protestant and Catholic exegesis much closer together.

Finally, the Bible was and continues to be returned to the people, either through its being read and preached about in the mass, through Bible studies in communitarian groups, or through individual reading. The Bible has played an extraordinary role in the emergence and ongoing life of Christian base communities throughout Latin America in the last two and a half decades. An enthusiastic encounter is occurring between the people and the biblical story. Freed from prefabricated dogmatic interpretations as well as from suffocating exegetical erudition monopolized by theologians, the Bible has taken on an impressive vitality in the lives and relationships of the people.

Protestantism, for its part, came to Latin America as the "religion of the book." For the transplanted churches that emerged from the migratory influx into a number of countries on the continent, the Bible was a means of internal edification. For the missionary churches, it was also a weapon to combat "pagan" Catholicism. Even today, Protestant Bible societies continue to supply the Latin American consumer market, although modern, accessible Catholic or ecumenical editions have become available.

Protestant use of the Bible in Latin America is increasingly vulnerable to two equally ominous tendencies. One is to repristinate the Protestant truths time and time again using biblical proof texts. Protestantism in its multiple variants has become so doctrinally codified that the Bible can no longer breathe freely but rather must serve to corroborate established doctrines. We Protestants may not have an authoritative magisterium or an infallible pope; we do have a dogmatist practice. The other tendency is at the extreme opposite: Tired of our dogmatic recapitulations and their biblical proof texts, we renounce the Bible as a resource for Christian practice. Clinging to the discoveries of the social sciences, we begin to think we can return the Bible to its past and forget about it.

From Luther we learned how to make discoveries and formulate doctrines about the gospel only on the basis of Scripture (*sola scriptura*). Is *sola scriptura* an element of dogmatism that we ought perhaps to send back to the sixteenth century with funereal honors? Or is there in this sixteenth-century insight some reservoir of spiritual good sense?

Luther and Scripture

The importance of the Bible in Luther's life   The fundamental significance the Bible and its study had for Luther's personal liberation, for his rediscovery of the gospel, and for the work of the Reformation, has been discussed in earlier chapters. Several other events and facts underscore this significance.

In 1521 at Worms, Luther was called before the imperial Diet. The excommunicated professor of Bible, who had gone to Worms to engage in dialogue about his teachings, was asked to recant his works. He requested and was given time to reflect. The next day in his reply,

Luther, speaking for "a cause of justice and of truth," made a distinction among three different kinds of books he had written.[1]

The first type, he said, consisted of expositions "in which I have discussed religious faith and morals simply and evangelically, so that even my enemies themselves are compelled to admit that these are useful, harmless, and clearly worthy to be read by Christians."[2] It would not be worthy to retract these. In the second category were books that attacked the pope and the papists "as those who both by their doctrines and very wicked examples have laid waste the Christian world with evil that affects the spirit and the body."[3] Their "unbelievable tyranny" was devouring the goods and inheritance of the German nation, Luther declared. If those were to be retracted, such tyranny would become "still more intolerable." The third type of books was directed against private persons and adversaries. Luther admitted to having been more acerbic than he needed to be, but even in this case, he believed he could not retract their contents. He declared himself ready, once again, to listen to the arguments against his works, and asked that whoever "is able, either high or low, bear witness, expose my errors, overthrowing them by the writings of the prophets and the evangelists. Once I have been taught I shall be quite ready to renounce every error, and I shall be the first to cast my books into the fire."[4]

At Worms, it was already clear that Luther did not recognize formal ecclesiastical authorities but instead marshalled arguments from Scripture. The secretary of the Diet told him that "those things which had been condemned and defined in councils" ought not to be called into question,[5] and asked him for a simple, unambiguous answer as to whether he wanted to recant or not. Luther responded,

> Since then your serene majesty and your lordships seek a simple answer, I will give it in this manner, neither horned nor toothed: Unless I am convinced by the testimony of the Scriptures or by clear reason (for I do not trust either in the pope or in councils alone, since it is well known that they have often erred and contradicted themselves), I am bound by the Scriptures I have quoted and my conscience is captive to the Word of God. I cannot and I will not retract anything, since it is neither safe nor right to go against conscience. May God help me![6]

[1] *LW* 32:109.
[2] Ibid.
[3] Ibid., 110.
[4] Ibid., 111.
[5] Ibid., 112.
[6] Ibid., 112–113.

Considering the concrete risk to his life, this episode reflects most dramatically Luther's disposition to depend on his conscience, guided by the Word of God as Luther found it in Scripture. The Diet at Worms condemned Luther and his teachings, and he lived the rest of his life as an imperial outlaw.

Although Luther was a biblical scholar throughout his life, he never believed he had arrived at a complete understanding of Scripture. He wrote that he had not "wholly understood even a single word of all of Scripture."[7] He had never "really understood the Ten Commandments."[8] He taught the book of Genesis for twelve years, always in a free and original way, always in light of the burning issues of his time—and always in hot pursuit of biblical sense. The last words he wrote, two days before he died, on February 16, 1546, were

> Nobody can understand Virgil in his *Bucolics* and *Georgics* unless he has first been a shepherd or a peasant for five years. Nobody understands Cicero in his letters unless he has been engaged in public affairs of some consequence for twenty years. Let nobody suppose that he has tasted the Holy Scriptures sufficiently unless he has ruled over the churches with the prophets for a hundred years. . . . We are beggars. That is true.[9]

The priesthood of all believers   Luther developed his doctrine of the priesthood of all believers in a treatise of a decidedly political stamp—*To the Christian Nobility of the German Nation Concerning the Reform of the Christian Estate* (1520). More important here than the fact that Luther derived Christians' political vocation from their "royal priesthood" is his assertion that the priesthood of all baptized believers required breaking the papal monopoly over the interpretation of the Bible. There are no masters of Scripture, Luther asserted, much less infallible interpreters—as the pope claimed to be—and even fewer if they learn nothing from Scripture in their whole lives.[10] The notion that it was solely up to the pope to interpret Scripture or to confirm its interpretation was "an outrageous fancied fable."[11] Luther made continuous use of the Bible to ground universal priesthood. "We ought to become bold and free on the authority of all these texts, and many others," Luther wrote.

[7]*WA* TR 2, 303, 5 (no. 204) [English translation by translator.]
[8]*WA* 45, 152, 26–27. [English translation by translator.]
[9]*LW* 54:476.
[10]*LW* 44:133–34.
[11]Ibid., 134.

We ought not to allow the Spirit of freedom (as Paul calls him [II Cor. 3:17]) to be frightened off by the fabrications of the popes, but we ought to march boldly forward and test all that they do, or leave undone, by our believing understanding of the Scriptures. We must compel the Romanists to follow not their own interpretation but a better one.[12]

However, Luther did not want to replace the tyrannical judgment of ecclesiastical authority with the arbitrary judgment of the individual believer. He made a point of linking the establishment of universal priesthood with the task of discernment in a communal framework, characterized by diversity of function. In his treatise *That a Christian Assembly or Congregation Has the Right and Power to Judge All Teaching and to Call, Appoint, and Dismiss Teachers, Established and Proven by Scripture* (1523),[13] he assigned to the Christian community the task of judging doctrine. The urgency with which he counseled the municipal political authorities to take education seriously, reflected in his treatise *To the Councilmen of All Cities in Germany That They Establish and Maintain Christian Schools* (1524),[14] was motivated in part by his commitment to the preparation of everyone— men and women—to read and understand Scripture. He also wrote a variety of works designed to help prepare pastors for their new task of preaching from Scripture.

Universal priesthood, Luther believed, was properly exercised neither through the mechanical repetition of biblical passages nor through arbitrary individual interpretation but rather through the ongoing effort made by the community, in all its diversity, to come to terms with the biblical message. This is the process through which the scriptural Word becomes clear.

Interpreting Scripture

The clarity of Scripture   Once Luther discovered the central theme of justification by grace and faith, he became convinced that the sense of Scripture was clear, not so much in the formal sense as orthodoxy came to understand it, but rather in the sense that Scripture

[12]Ibid., 135.
[13]*LW* 39:305–14.
[14]*LW* 45:347–78.

reveals its basic content to those who struggle with it. In the historical retrospective of the *Preface to the Complete Edition of Luther's Latin Writings* (1545), Luther added this to the story of his liberating discovery of justification by faith: "There a totally other face of the entire Scripture showed itself to me. Thereupon I ran through the Scriptures from memory. I also found in other terms [besides the "righteousness of God"—*au.*] an analogy, as, the work of God, that is, what God does in us, the power of God, with which he makes us strong, the wisdom of God, with which he makes us wise, the strength of God, the salvation of God, the glory of God."[15]

Having discovered the evangelical center of the Scripture, Luther also found that Scripture itself changed its meaning and revealed its meaning: The attributes of God were no longer qualities of God that threaten us but rather were expressions of God's liberating action in our favor. This discovery impelled Luther into an even more intense examination of Scripture and into a simplification of his exegetical method. In accordance with the hermeneutic of the Middle Ages that Luther had inherited, the biblical texts were to be analyzed in four senses: the literal or grammatical, the allegorical or spiritual, the tropological or parenetic, and the anagogical or eschatological.

Luther began to concentrate more and more on the literal sense of the texts: "The Holy Spirit is the simplest writer in heaven and on earth. That is why his words could have no more than the one simplest meaning, which we call the written one, or the literal meaning of the tongue."[16] His method had little in common with later literalism or fundamentalism; rather its purpose was to pay attention to the meaning of the text itself, which carries with it its own spiritual, parenetic, or eschatological overtones. Artificial spiritualizing is unnecessary. Luther's emphasis on the literal meaning united him, for his own specific reasons, with the humanists' return to the sources and to the study of ancient languages. Knowledge of the original languages, Hebrew or Greek, should take precedence over any translation. However, this by no means made translations of the Bible superfluous, because they were the means of putting the Bible into the hands of the common people.

The art of translating   With his translation of the Bible, Luther realized one of his most significant works and set an indelible stamp

---

[15]*LW* 34:337.
[16]*LW* 39:178.

on the modern German language. His commitment was not to the
letter but to the sense of the text and its translation into the speech
of the people. Criticized for having introduced into his German translation of Romans 3:28 the word "only" ("... the human being is justified
without the works of the law, only through faith"), Luther called his
critics asses, and adduced linguistic and material arguments to support
his version. The particle "only" simply makes the adversative sentence
explicit, he declared, and is the way people talk in any case:

> We do not have to inquire of the literal Latin, how we are to speak German,
> as these asses do. Rather we must inquire about this of the mother in the
> home, the children on the street, the common man in the marketplace.
> We must be guided by their language, the way they speak, and do our
> translating accordingly. That way they will understand it and recognize
> that we are speaking German to them.[17]

The canon within the canon   Luther absolutized neither the
book nor the letter of Scripture. As essential as Scripture might be, as
much as it might be a vehicle for the Spirit of God, as worthy of respect
as even its indecipherable passages might be (like a sun behind the
clouds),[18] Luther argued, even more decisive are the movement of
God's Spirit and the living proclamation of the Word.

Luther's vigorous advocacy for the exclusivity and sufficiency of
Scripture was rooted in his conviction that ecclesiastical dogmatisms
and ceremonial traditions were strangling the live proclamation of the
Word. But Scripture was for him a kind of emergency treatment: We
must scrutinize God's Word in its written form because we are weak.
Luther believed this so firmly that he could describe Scripture as "a
serious decline and a lack of the Spirit."[19]

He defined the church by saying that "the whole life and substance
of the church is in the Word of God," and added immediately, "I am
not speaking about the written gospel, but rather about the spoken."[20]
Luther recalled that Christ wrote nothing and on this basis concluded
that the New Testament was more a living voice than a written text.[21]
In a sermon in 1523, he says,

---

[17]LW 35:189.
[18]WA 8, 239, 16–18.
[19]LW 52:206.
[20]WA 7, 721, 12–13. [English translation by translator.]
[21]Ibid., 10/I/2, 35, 1–2; see also LW 52:205–06.

Gospel means nothing else than a preaching and a crying out of the grace and the mercy of God, merited and conquered by the Lord Christ by means of his death. And it is not what is found in books and what is written in letters; rather, it is a voice that resounds in all the world and will, pray God, be shouted and heard in all places.[22]

With this perspective Luther gained freedom—relative, but rare—in relation to the biblical texts. Once the center of the Scripture—the Good News of the grace of God in Jesus Christ, received in faith—was found, then isolated passages, even isolated books, of the Bible could be measured in relation to this center. Luther did not think much of the Epistle to the Hebrews or of Revelation, and even less of the Letter of James—that "epistle of straw," he called it. Revelation lent itself to sectarian interpretations, he thought, and the Letter of James served the church as ideological legitimation for its contention that prescribed good works like the purchase of indulgences were required for salvation. Luther was tempted to exclude those books from the canon, but his respect for Scripture did not permit him to do so. In this way, he maintained a sense of its liberating relevance in new situations. (For example, it is obvious that the ethical advice and social criticism of the Letter of James are very much to the point when the abuse of justification by faith leads to ethical passivity in situations of social oppression.) The correct interpretation of Scripture, departing from a center, does not begin and end with particular books; it is an ongoing task involving all biblical passages.

Consequently, Luther could move only in a hermeneutical circle that was simultaneously combative and liberated. On the one hand:

Against all the declarations of the fathers (of the church), against the art and the word of all the angels, human beings, and the Devil, I lift up the Scripture and the Gospel ... That is where I am, that is where I am boastful, that is where I am proud and say: the Word of God is greater than anything for me.[23]

On the other hand was the criterion by which to interpret the Bible: *was Christum treibt* [what preaches Christ]. "That which does not teach Christ is not apostolic," Luther declares, "even though St. Peter

---

[22]WA 12, 259. [English translation by translator.]
[23]WA 10/II, 256, 26—32. [English translation by translator.]

or Paul might teach it; conversely, that which teaches Christ is apostolic, even if Judas, Annas, Pilate, or Herod do it." And a bit earlier: "In this all the holy books concur: they all preach and promote Christ; this is also the correct key by which to censor all the books: do they promote Christ or not."[24]

In the end, it is impossible to find a more radical expression of opposition to legalistic and literalistic understandings of the Bible than this one: "Therefore, if the adversaries press the Scriptures against Christ, we urge Christ against the Scriptures."[25]

Luther and the Hermeneutical Problem

It is clear that Luther did not have the hermeneutical last word. It is equally clear that, whatever the considerable merits of his hermeneutical conceptions, we cannot simply return to them today.

Since the sixteenth century, the hermeneutical focus has changed many times. Protestant orthodoxy emphasized the dogmatic necessities of doctrine. Pietism spiritualized the interpretation of Scripture, asking "What does it say to me?" Rationalist historicism, in search of the historical Jesus, thematized methodological distrust of dogma. The failure of this project provoked in dialectic theology the recognition of biblical texts' kerygmatic character. Barth, for example, underscored the need for the interpreter to allow him or herself to be carried along by that to which the biblical account bears witness. In this sense, Barth reiterated the discovery of the Reformation: The biblical text should be searched in terms of its own intentions, and it is up to the interpreter to investigate it with tireless and faithful dedication.

On the other hand, historical analysis has helped us to understand the original setting of biblical passages or texts. Can James and Romans, formally contradictory texts in relation to justification, be reread in such a way that these texts might illuminate one another? Luther's intuition about preserving the letter of James for the future was indeed "providential," even if he himself was only able to find things to attack there. Using the historical-critical method, the specific historical contexts of these two letters can be illuminated. Paul was battling legalism

[24]*WA* DB 7, 384, 25–27.
[25]*LW* 34:112, Thesis 49.

as a means of access to salvation, while James was dealing with a community that had accommodated itself, that was using justification by faith as a pretext for its inertia. Luther undoubtedly had good reasons to reject the Roman church's demand for "good works" like veneration of relics, pilgrimages, and purchase of indulgences as necessary to gain salvation. In the Latin American historical context, marked by social oppression for which the Christian churches bear much responsibility, the prophetic testimony of James is crucial; at the same time, the gratuitousness of salvation in Christ, which is for Paul essential, must not be underplayed.

In general, the hermeneutical effort during the last decades has been drawn to the problem of the distance between the biblical text of the past and the interpreter's present reality. Luther does offer some guidance here when, for example, he sees Scripture as a vehicle for the living and present proclamation of the gospel or when he argues that biblical texts must be translated in the language of the people, in their homes, in the streets, and in the marketplace.

But it was considerably easier for Luther in his day than it is for us today to claim for himself the correct interpretation and to ascribe to his adversaries the false one. Luther's hermeneutical circle unfolded from the general text toward its interior or center, that is, toward the past, toward its constitutive event, Christ. Modern hermeneutical circles work, to a large degree, from the text forward, toward the present reality or, more to the point, from our situation toward the text. No one comes to the text unencumbered by preconceptions that influence one's reading and that need to become conscious before the reading can achieve real relevance or an approximate objectivity.

So, for example, Bultmann starts from a preunderstanding that is given with the existential situation of the interpreter. The existentially situated interpreter studies the biblical text, whose message should yield up its meaning in terms that are relevant for the existential situation. The gospel will be Good News of the victory in the cross of Christ over the fatal preoccupation with life's transitoriness and limitations. The method of Juan Luis Segundo is formally similar, in that it treats as its point of departure the historical-social reality, and in so doing, fosters the exegetical and ideological suspicion needed to study the biblical text and to extract from it the revolutionary dimensions that the experience of the historical-social situation requires. For Paul Ricoeur, suspicion—of interests, desires, and will that exist prior to the reading of the text—is a key hermeneutical instrument by means of which to ask the questions that unmask and destabilize, such as the questions posed by Marx, Nietzsche, and Freud.

The Bible is not a monolith; on the contrary, it is part of a life process, of an historical process. We have on the one hand, a history of methods that attempt "scientifically" to approach the sense of Scripture; on the other—and this is much more important—we have the concrete and contextualized impact Scripture makes on persons, communities, churches, and even historical eras. The scientific method is valid or not to the degree that it reflects and touches the historical process that is going on.

The emphasis Luther gives to the literal sense of the biblical text is relevant not because it arrives at the absolute sense of Scripture (which we know does not exist) but rather because it locates its meaning relevantly, in a particular historical-ecclesial context. Luther's position reflects his discovery of personal meaning for faith and a critique of the institution that held the monopoly on the interpretation of Scripture: the papacy. This discovery is also hermeneutically liberating because it unchains the matter of what the biblical text might mean. The question begins to be raised as to what the text really has to say, not in order to reach an absolute and immutable interpretation but rather in order to combat the interpretive judgment of the ecclesiastical power that supports itself—"ideologically," we could say—by using the medieval hermeneutical method of the four senses, originally a method of great vitality.

Ultimately, Luther refuses to emphasize only the literal sense of Scripture and the principle of its self-interpretation; he maintains that Scripture cannot be imprisoned by any one method. In this way—obviously, without knowing the structuralist interpretation—Luther leaves space open for new methods and their resulting interpretations. When the method of the "literal sense" was absolutized and lost Luther's insistence on the utter centrality of listening for the "living voice of the gospel"—as happened in Protestant orthodoxy—it became vulnerable to sharp criticism.

None of the hermeneutical concerns mentioned earlier, which emerge out of our situation and are directed toward the biblical text, can be discarded; none of them is treated adequately by Luther. Even though the experience of Christian base communities has demonstrated that even today the biblical text can become relevant through immediate analogies drawn from current situations, the hermeneutical problem has a theoretical dimension that cannot be neglected.

It is not accidental that some of the most creative and serious study of the Bible is occurring within communities that are consciously involved in a transformative social-historical praxis. On the Latin American continent, profoundly wounded by systems of oppression, the suffering of people who are united in their struggle for liberation is an unavoidable hermeneutical arena for all Bible reading.

What Can Luther Offer?

First, the relevance of the Bible lies in its use and not in its mere possession. It is a living word when it is the object of study *and* when there is a living out of the Word of God. And Luther's protests against interpretation monopolized by some ecclesiastical entity and against a sterile dogmatic literalism remain perfectly valid today.

Second, Luther believed that the Bible had its own authority, by means of God's Spirit, which takes precedence over the authority of the biblical interpreter. Given the failure of the nineteenth-century historicists to reconstruct the life of Jesus and knowing that we are conditioned by our preunderstandings, our desires, and our interests, might we not strive to develop a finer sense of the theological affirmation that the biblical story and message become relevant by the power of their content rather than of their interpretation?

Third, while we cannot ignore modern expressions of the hermeneutical circle that move back and forth between contemporary reality and the biblical text, we ought not file away completely Luther's version, which moves from the Scripture as a whole toward its constitutive center, and back again. What matters is the realm of God manifested in Christ and made reality in our historical situation. The Bible is the means: forward, to our historical reality; back, to the life and activity of Jesus.

Fourth, these perceptions lend an incredible and special freedom and life to working with the Bible. In the hands of the people (as, in good measure, was true during the Reformation), in proclamation and study, and in the free search for new discoveries, the Bible goes on giving off its captivating perfume and exercising its transformative attraction. The Scripture—*sola scriptura*—is place and means for the liberating activity of God's Spirit. It strengthens with hope a people in struggle. The Bible moves from a dead letter to an instrument of life.

5

The Church

The Church in Latin America

Christianity arrived in Latin America via the Catholic church as part of the process of conquest and colonization by the Spanish and the Portuguese. Although there were always some prophetic and independent voices within it, the church as an institution came to the New World aligned with the state and with the Iberian crowns' designs of conquest and domination. Under the system of *patronato* (patronage), priests and missionaries became royal functionaries. In the service of the crown, the cross allied itself with the sword. This is what came to be called "Christendom."

According to the terms of this project, the Portuguese and the Spanish were to fulfill the historic task of expanding the frontiers of their own civilization, way of life, culture, and belief, embracing other conquered lands and peoples. In exchange for their superior civilization and the true Christian faith, they considered it entirely legitimate that they should receive—if possible voluntarily, but if necessary by force of arms—the wealth and labor of the peoples they conquered and converted.

In this way, the Catholic church and the Christianity it represented constituted itself a collaborator within a larger system of domination and oppression. Parallel to this historical development, a broad network of "popular" Christian practices and beliefs began to take shape as an expression of the suffering of the people and their determination to survive and resist domination. If the Catholic church today can speak of a Christian Latin America, this is surely the very ambiguous result of five centuries of history. The Christianity that arrived with

57

the conquerors sank deep roots in the peoples of Latin America. These masses articulate their faith not in an orthodox way but informally, often syncretistically, retaining legacies of the faith of both Native and African American peoples.

Vatican II (1962 to 1965) rejected the triumphalist vision of the church as a fundamentally juridical, institutional, pyramidal body, concentrated in the hierarchy, and substituted a definition of the church as a mystery of God, with the people of God taking precedence over the hierarchy. With this step, popular Christianity gained its freedom; its legitimacy was recognized. Base Christian communities are the most vigorous expression of this new ecclesiastical reality in Latin America. They are communities that live their faith—the "people's faith"—in the midst of the experiences, hopes, and struggles of the common people. A Christianity of the people, a Christianity of survival and resistance, has entered the struggle for liberation within history.

The transformation of a church of domination into a church of liberation is remarkable. It is no surprise that this church meets with increasing resistance. Even at Puebla (1979),[1] an attempt was made by the church hierarchy to bind the Christian base communities more tightly to the hierarchy. The bishops were both recognizing the legitimacy of the Christian base communities and setting the stage to control and discipline them. The Latin American (Catholic) Bishops Conference (CELAM), too, increasingly supported by directives from Rome, tries to rein in the vitality of the base communities. At the same time, a good number of Catholic bishops and even national and continent-wide episcopal groups have become voices for those who have no voice. The significance of the change within key Catholic circles from a perspective of domination to one of liberation cannot be minimized.

If we look at Latin American Protestantism, especially to the Protestantism of transplantation or of immigration, we can see a contrasting dynamic. Almost all the German immigrants who came to Brazil beginning in 1824, for example, were members of exploited or marginalized groups. (Later, people from the rising capitalist classes, who espoused liberal ideals but were defeated in the Revolution of 1848, also migrated, especially to Chile.) They were rural day laborers or small farmers, who lacked the conditions even for subsistence as the

---

[1]CELAM held its second assembly at Puebla, Mexico, in 1979. Its first assembly in Medellín, Colombia (1968), had given strong support to the development of the Christian base communities.

process of industrialization got under way in Germany. The Hanseatic city of Hamburg took advantage of the wave of immigration to empty its prisons. Despite the difficulties these immigrants had to surmount— when the governments of the countries they went to failed to fulfill their promises to them, for example, or because they were marginalized for social, cultural, or religious reasons—there was much to be grateful for: a new land to cultivate, the possibility of building a life. To return to Germany seems not to have been either a temptation or a dream.

Among the most agreeable aspects of their move across the Atlantic was the opportunity to organize autonomous religious communities, free from the oversight of the state churches, which were dominated by the territorial German governments (a legacy from the time of the Reformation). For a long time, the immigrants resisted the formation of any kind of supraparochial church organization like synods. The Evangelical Church of the Lutheran Confession in Brazil finally constituted itself in 1949; even today, there are sharp reservations about and resistance to the central church apparatus.

For the same reasons, the new church communities were defined by a sharp sense of introversion. Their orienting principles were to preserve the faith and to attend to the religious needs of the community. The missionary perspective and the concern about the evangelical presence in Brazilian society were virtually ignored. The church institution as it finally emerged was accepted, more than anything, for the service it provided and provides directly to the congregations, for example, in preparing pastors. Challenges to tasks involving political mission are often coldly received, or may even be explicitly condemned.

Almost all the Protestant mission churches, for their part, came to Latin America from the United States. Because of their missionary character, they formed minority communities inclined to polemicize against the surrounding (Catholic) medium. Besides the Protestant faith, they offered the liberal vision of American development capitalism or of American manifest destiny. Here and there, the effort attracted small middle classes in the ascendant. Protestant communities scarcely existed among the poor majorities.

This Protestantism developed a critique of the traditional oligarchic, semifeudal stratification in Latin America. In this way, it contributed to the modernization of society in an urban setting and to the adoption of liberal ideals, like providing solid education for the middle classes. In general, however, when confronted with the radical liberation of the oppressed Latin American masses, the critique evaporated.

Instead, this brand of Protestantism then stayed with the bourgeois, developmentalist model, an option facilitated by the fact that Latin American economies were dominated by international capitalism. Protestantism thus lost much of its potential for renewal, leading in large measure to its stagnation.

In contrast, Pentecostalism grew impressively in many countries, especially among the poor. Its form of worship is more congenial to the soul of the people, serving as a medium of expression and, in its way, as a response to the basic inner aspirations of the Latin American populations. The practices of healing also respond to one of the basic physical needs, namely health care, for a population who cannot afford to pay for expensive medical care. Its ecclesiology is of extreme vitality, as much in its worship as in its sense of mission. It shows an extraordinary mobility. The Pentecostal church is the only religious group that really has managed to accompany those many millions of Latin Americans who have migrated during the last few decades.

The great popularity of Pentecostalism is a challenge to attend to its liberating potential. At the same time, its role is very ambiguous: Is it liberating or alienating? Does it contribute to the transformation of unjust social structures or to their perpetuation? To its predominantly dualistic theology and practice, the political arena appears demonic and, therefore, should be abandoned by Christians. It is, however, a strong movement among the poor, with a potential for liberating practice. Only the future will tell us whether or not Pentecostalism will be an instrument of domination or of liberation.

As we turn back to Luther with this context in mind, we will of course not find the answers to these questions. Perhaps, however, we can find in his work some guideposts that could help us even today in developing an appropriate church theology and practice within this context.

The Church in Luther

Defining the Church

"Thank God, a seven-year-old child knows what the church is, namely, holy believers and sheep who hear the voice of their Shepherd."[2] These words of Luther provide a concise and apt synthesis of

---

[2]The Smalcald Articles, in *The Book of Concord*, op. cit., 315.

his ecclesiology. Only these two elements enter into the definition of church: the congregation of the believers (sheep that listen) and the Word of God (the voice of their shepherd).

The elements Luther excluded from the definition are also meaningful. The definition that appeared in the Smalcald Articles explicitly rejected ecclesiastical ceremonies and liturgical symbols as constitutive of the church. Also excluded were institutional elements—except the "congregation" or coming together of believers—and the predominance of an ecclesiastical hierarchy. According to Luther, the point of departure for defining the church was not the general, universal organization but rather the local community. And even in this definition of 1537, dated twenty years after the Reformation began, there was no sign of denominational confessionalism.

Let us look at two key elements of Luther's ecclesiology: first, his understanding of the church as the People of God, or the congregation of the saints:

> We shall this time confine ourselves simply to the Children's Creed, which says, "I believe in one holy Christian church, the communion of saints." Here the creed clearly indicates what the church is, namely, a communion of saints, that is, a crowd or assembly of people who are Christians and holy, which is called a Christian holy assembly, or church. . . . Church is nothing but an assembly of people, though they probably were heathens and not Christians. Now there are many peoples in the world; the Christians, however, are a people with a special call and are therefore called not just ecclesia, "church," or "people," but *sancta catholica Christiana* . . . Thus the "holy Christian church" is synonymous with a Christian and holy people or, as one is also wont to express it, with "holy Christendom," or "whole Christendom." The Old Testament uses the term "God's people."[3]

For Luther, the church was originally and fundamentally the community of those who shared faith in Christ. "Community" is the New Testament term for what in the Old Testament is called "people of God." The church comprised God's people, Luther contended, not the pastors, the bishops, or the pope: ". . . the pope is no people, much less a holy Christian people. So too the bishops, priests, and monks are not holy, Christian people. . . ."[4] Where there was only one baptism, only one gospel, only one people, there, too, all were equally Christians,

---

[3]*LW* 41:143–44.
[4]Ibid., 144.

all equally priests. No member, whatever his or her function, could have an authority greater than that of God's people. In translating the New Testament, Luther used the word "community," preferring it to "church," a term he set aside because it generally connoted hierarchy.

Luther also noted the specificity of God's people:

> In truth, the gospel comes before the bread (Holy Supper) and baptism, as the one most certain and noble sign of the church, because it is only through the gospel that the church is conceived, formed, nourished, born, educated, fed, clothed, ornamented, strengthened, prepared, and sustained. In a word: The whole life and substance of the church is in the Word of God.[5]

Or:

> For the church was born by the word of promise through faith and by this same word is fed and preserved. That is to say, it is the promises of God that make the church, and not the church that makes the promise of God. For the Word of God is incomparably superior to the church, and in this Word the church, being a creature, has nothing to decree, ordain, or make, but only to be decreed, ordained, and made.[6]

Or, finally: "In fact, the church is the child of the gospel."[7]

For Luther, the church is brought forth and shaped by the Word of God. Without it, the community would be a community but not the Christian and holy community; a people, but not the people of God. Without the Word, the church would be nothing, even if it had the showiest buildings, the most effective organization, and the most dynamic program of activities. On the other hand, where the Word of God is, there the church is—even if the community is weak and small.

Making Distinctions

The internal church and the external church Luther claimed that the gospel reformed and renewed the church. He never planned or pretended to form a perfect church; in fact, he never wanted to leave the Catholic church. Despite being excommunicated, until the end of his life he never thought of himself as the founder of a

---

[5]WA 7, 721, 9–13. [English translation by translator.]
[6]LW 36:107.
[7]WA 2, 430, 6–7.

denominational church, but rather simply as a pastor of the universal church of Christ, in Wittenberg. "In the first place," he wrote,

> I ask that men make no reference to my name; let them call themselves Christians, not Lutherans. What is Luther? After all, the teaching is not mine. Neither was I crucified for anyone. St. Paul, in I Corinthians 3, would not allow the Christians to call themselves Pauline or Petrine, but Christian. How then should I ... come to have men call the children of God by my wretched name? Not so, my dear friends; let us abolish all party names and call ourselves Christians, after him whose teaching we hold ... I neither am nor want to be anyone's master. I hold, together with the universal church, the one universal teaching of Christ, who is our only master.[8]

It is clear that we have not escaped the unhappy historical contingency of the formation of a Lutheran church and other denominational churches. It should be equally clear, however, that any Lutheran who is not ecumenical is abusing the name of Luther. Luther never allowed himself to be dominated by the sectarianism that meant to separate the "saints and saved" from the "impure and condemned."

Seeking both the reformation of the church and freedom from sectarianism, Luther distinguished between the internal church and the external church, the church as creature of the Word and the church as human organization, the church as object of faith and the manifest church. Just as the believer is at once justified and sinner, so the church is also at once justified and sinful, justified by the Word that constitutes it and sinful because of the perversion of the will of God imprinted on it by those who form it: justified ones, but sinners. Whoever attempts to guarantee the institutional purity of the church by separating out only the justified inevitably and immediately transforms it into a false church. The movement toward the true church is not a work that concludes, but rather a struggle in permanent process, a struggle between the Word of Christ and Christ's realm against the reality of evil that also exists in the midst of the church.

This conflict will not be resolved within time as we know it but rather in the consummation of time, when the realization of the Realm of God makes the church superfluous. Until then, we will always have the external church as an imperfect expression of the internal church. Only the internal church will give the external church its dignity, but the internal church also will be the source of permanent critique.

[8]*LW* 45:70–71.

The visibility and the invisibility of the church   There are a number of passages in which Luther emphasizes the invisibility of the church. He points out, for example, that the church is confessed—in the third article of the Apostles' Creed; as such, it is invisible, for what is seen is clearly not held in faith. Once more we note Luther's strong institutional critique:

> For what is believed is neither physical nor visible. All of us can see the external Roman church. That is why it cannot be the true church, which is believed and which is a community or assembly of the saints in faith. But no one can see who is holy or who believes.[9]

There were occasions—and obviously there still are—in which the meaning of the concept of the invisibility of the church was perverted. German Lutheran theologies of the nineteenth century, for example, strongly accentuated the invisibility of the church in order to keep the external institution of a bourgeois state church out of critical reach. As absolutized, the concept of the invisibility of the church was stripped of its critical power. The fact is that Luther himself used the concept to describe the profound nature of the church, not to spiritualize or protect it. Luther spoke in much the same way of the signs of the church—not as a fixed number nor in an absolute sense. He could summarize them all by referring to the Word of God: where the Word was found and was acting, he argued, there is the church. But he could also extend the list of signs to include not only the Word but also the sacraments, ministries, prayer, and the experience of suffering and the cross.[10]

All these signs, as manifestations of the Word, are also visible characteristics of the church. What remains invisible is its ultimate nature. For this, Luther used the expression "hidden" instead of the term "invisible."[11] The church is hidden in the signs. In keeping with the nature of God's own revelation and salvation, moreover, the signs are weak and small. Just as the power of God is hidden in the cross of Christ—but revealed to faith—so the church of God becomes actual and active in the improbable signs of the Word, the sacraments, prayer, and the cross.

[9]*LW* 39:75.
[10]*LW* 41:164–65.
[11]*WA* 7, 722, 5 and 8.

The church as a place of healing Luther frequently admonished the community to love those in need and to protect the vulnerable. According to I Cor. 12, there is a mutual responsibility of the members of the Christian community as the Body of Christ. For Luther, Paul's image of the body, with its many members and its particular concern for the weaker ones, was an apt metaphor for the Christian community. The whole human body concerns itself with the least of its suffering members. This is what happens—or should happen—in the Christian community as the Body of Christ: When the smallest member suffers, all suffer with and care for that member.

In this way, in precariousness and in love, the church is an instrument that battles against evil. It does not claim to be the Realm of God, but it can serve the Realm of God. "The church is the inn and the infirmary," he wrote, "for those who are sick and in need of being made well. But heaven is the palace of the healthy and the righteous."[12] The church is a place of healing. The terrestrial palaces may belong to the powerful who know nothing of the love and the cross of Christ; the church of Christ does not walk within its chambers.

One of Luther's hymns expresses much better all that I have been trying to say:

Ah God, from heaven look down and view;
Let it thy pity waken;
Behold thy saints how very few!
We wretches are forsaken.
Thy word they will not grant it right,
And faith is thus extinguished quite
Amongst the sons of Adam.

They teach a cunning false and fine,
In their own wits they found it;
Their heart in one doth not combine,
Upon God's word well grounded.
One chooses this, the other that;
Endless division they are at,
And yet they keep smooth faces.

Therefore said God: "I must be up;
My poor ones ill are faring;
Their sighs crowd up to Zion's top,
My ear their cry is hearing.

[12]*LW* 25:263.

My healing word shall speedily
With comfort fill them, fresh and free,
And strength be to the needy."

Silver that seven times is tried
With fire, is found the purer;
God's word the same test will abide,
It still comes out the surer.
It shall by crosses proved be;
Men shall its strength and glory see
Shine strong upon the nations.[13]

Luther's Ecclesiology and the Church in Latin America

Leonardo Boff wrote a book with the wonderful title *Ecclesiogenesis* and a subtitle that almost implies setting up a global project: *The Base Communities Reinvent the Church*.[14] His brother Clodovis Boff has written of the Christian base communities as creators of a new type of Christian without precedent in history.[15] While his conclusion may suffer a bit from the exaggeration of enthusiasm, there is little doubt that the emergence and the expansion of Christian base communities on the Latin American continent represents the most significant impulse of ecclesiological renewal of our time.

In this context, it is well worth remarking on the revolutionary force implicit in Luther's ecclesiology, with its communitarian emphasis, its drive toward liberation from institutional tutelage, its conviction that ecclesiastical structure is both reformable and meant for service; its preference for the mark of the cross (and the weakness manifested there), and the primacy of the Word of God.

We must also note the freeing of the church from its role as guardian of the dominant political order—a liberation that was only tentative and not effective. At a particular historical moment, Luther accommodated himself to the secular territorial authority. He saw this as a temporary measure at a stage of transition. But what was for him temporary became institutionalized: The territorial churches became

---

[13]*LW* 53:226—28. The *Lutheran Book of Worship* does not include this hymn.
[14]Translated by Robert R. Barr (Maryknoll, N.Y.: Orbis Books, 1986).
[15]"CEBs e práticas de liberação," *Revista Eclesiástica Brasileira* 40, no. 160 (1980): 595–625.

allied with and subject to their respective princes. This development carried with it the inevitable loss of solidarity with the weak. The community of believers, once again under the aegis of an ecclesiastical institution, received religious services from this institution, whose executive officials were the pastors.

Lutherans and other Protestant heirs of the Reformation legacy have often played out, in subsequent generations, the worst tendencies of these sixteenth-century developments. Lutheran immigrants to Brazil were content, as we saw, to be freed from their state churches in Germany. Generally, however, they expected to be served by a church structure often subservient to the dominant local powers instead of being a community of mission and liberating service in solidarity with those on the margins. The reformation of the church, in fact, remains to be accomplished.

Christian base communities are an expression of this possibility of reformation. They are characterized by a living out of faith, communicated at the same time through worship and through the search for liberation within human history. How far they can continue to develop within the Catholic church, given its tendencies toward institutional and hierarchical discipline, is an open question. But their vitality emphatically suggests that pessimism is out of place.

For Latin American Protestants, another question emerges: Can the experience of the Christian base communities become a widespread reality in our churches? The obvious difficulties have to do with both demographic and historical factors. The Roman Catholicism of the Latin American popular majorities has deep and ubiquitous roots throughout the continent. Within this ethos, it is relatively easy to organize communities that join worship with the daily practice of the faith in concrete experience. Moreover, the Catholic church as an institution can tolerate with greater facility a two-track pastoral ministry, one of "popular" groups and the other of upper-class groups, often called "minorities" in Latin America.

Protestants, on the other hand, are distinctly in the minority in Latin America. Almost all local Protestant communities are constituted solely by middle-class and, to a degree, upper-class people. Energies within the churches are taken up in strengthening the structure of the congregation and in defining its reason for being. The celebration of the common faith, not experience or daily communal reality, is the unifying connection among members. Traditional Protestant modes of distinguishing and relating faith and politics only add to the difficulties we face in developing a more adequate relation between our church communities and the political and economic realities that require our response as Christians.

Clodovis Boff has argued that Christian base communities have played an important political role during a critical period of recent Latin American history.[16] As communities of faith, they have also often been the only space within which the people could organize during key historical moments. The most mature Christian base communities have discovered that they are especially and distinctively spaces of faith, in which their members are strengthened to act within their own popular organizations beyond the bounds of the church community. Often but not always, there is a close personal and collective connection between the two groups.

What are the special tasks of the ecclesial community, tasks that cannot be delegated? Clodovis Boff notes these: the celebration of the faith and education in the faith. Protestants might call these worship and Christian education, and would probably add proclamation and mission to the list of tasks. Boff might omit these latter elements on the unexamined assumption that all of Latin America is already Christian and believing—the "strange fruit" of Christendom's colonial project.

Worship, Christian education, mission—celebration of the faith, education in the faith, spreading of the faith—these elements form the structure of the church community that finds the source of its life in the gospel of Jesus Christ and its historical definition in the struggle for the liberation of those who have been made poor. Church: the poor people of God.

[16]Ibid., 604. There is a remarkable parallel in the role played by the predominantly Catholic Christian base communities in Latin America under the military dictatorships and by predominantly Lutheran congregations and groups in the former German Democratic Republic under the Stalinist dictatorship. In both cases, the Christian community constituted a highly significant space of freedom; in both cases, a broad grassroots and then mass movement toward democracy eventually developed. In both cases, the question of the identity and role of the Christian community arose anew in a rather critical way under the new situation of democratic freedom.

6

Interpreting the "Two Kingdoms"

The question of church and politics has particular urgency and priority because it requires us to focus on the well-being of specific persons, of oppressed people—of all of humanity, finally. At this moment in Latin American history, we live with the legacy of centuries of dependence, domination, and oppression; at the same time, we are also seeking liberation. The church cannot evade the question of its relation to political reality. It cannot pretend neutrality.

Throughout Latin American history, the church has been predominantly an instrument of domination. In this historic hour, can we be an instrument of liberation? It is an open question, to which only the historical process will give the answer. But when the church is willing to enter into its prophetic mission, to engage in transformative action, it is drawn into the conflicts that characterize our present situation, both outside and within the churches.

The view that a Christian should not get involved in politics—and that certainly the church should not—is not exclusively Lutheran. With variations, the concept is widely held among all the churches, including the Roman Catholic. But it was within the Lutheran tradition that the so-called doctrine of the two kingdoms arose; in this tradition, too, it has been used explicitly to legitimate political noninvolvement.

But do Luther's own formulation and argument support such an interpretation?

Church and State Under the Rule of God

The Two Realms of God's Activity

The dichotomous dualism between church and state cannot be legitimately ascribed to Luther. It is true that he drew a distinction of competencies between one and the other, but he neither separated nor defined them as autonomous entities. The distinction seemed to him indispensable. His purpose was very clear—to stand against the corruption of the church, which had become a temporal and political power. This emerges as early as 1517, in the Ninety-five Theses, in which Luther condemns the traffic in indulgences. The church, he argues in the theses, must offer the free forgiveness of God in Christ and must not take advantage of it as a source of enrichment.

This same distinction is very clearly stated in *To the Christian Nobility of the German Nation Concerning the Reform of the Christian Estate* (1520),[1] in which he levels radical criticisms against the political power of popes and bishops, against the system of feudal ecclesiastical properties, against the civil jurisprudence of the church, against its complicated and diverse fiscal system, and so on. All this created, in the name of the gospel, a concrete system of exploitation, Luther argued.

At the same time, Luther dignifies the social and political office in its broadest sense, even and especially for Christians. In addressing himself to the Christian nobility, Luther insists that their political function does not emerge autonomously and arbitrarily but from their universal priesthood as baptized Christians. As Christians called to political office, therefore, they ought to carry out the necessary economic, political, and social reforms of the German nation. Luther also responds positively to questions about the legitimacy and necessity of Christians' assuming public jobs in law, education, and the military.

Luther never meant to make the church and the state autonomous entities. It was the responsibility of the political authorities to achieve economic, political, and social reforms that would also affect the church; and it was the task of the church to confront the political authorities with God's will. The so-called two kingdoms can be distinguished regarding their tasks and their means, but they overlap in

[1]*LW* 44:123–217.

time and space. Furthermore, they have a common foundation—God is the Lord of both—and a common goal—human well-being.

Church and state limit and bind each other reciprocally. The state limits and regulates the church as a social institution (for example, in matters of property); the church proclaims God's will to the state (for example, criticizing its arbitrariness or calling on it to work for social, political, and economic transformation). Luther himself felt compelled to address the political authorities often. Whether his economic, political, and social demands were wise or tragic—and there were demands that fell into each category—the reformer could never be accused of, and never sought, political neutrality or abstention.

When Luther talks about "secular authorities," he is focusing on functions, not on an autonomous political office. "Secularization" of the political sphere in the sense of the modern liberal separation between church and state was not within his conceptual framework. Luther makes his distinction within the concept of "Christendom"; in this sense, he still lives under the legacy of the medieval system. He asks the German nobility to concern themselves with the improvement of the *Christian* estate. His proposals for education, which he calls on the state, particularly on the city authorities, to implement, may involve a new, basically humanist, pedagogy. But he wants *Christian* education. The foundation for the teaching should be the Bible, and the teacher's work belongs to the spiritual realm.

Would Latin American liberation theology be antagonistic to Luther's vision? It has often been thought so. And it is true that they have taken different paths, because their starting points are different. Taking into account their historical differences, however, they have similar objectives, not least of all in the matter under discussion here.

One elementary and very well-known aspect of Latin American liberation theology is its insistence on overcoming the distinction between the natural and the supernatural planes. Liberation theologians affirm that there is only one historical process, marked by antagonisms, conflicts, and transformations, in which Christians participate through their experience and faith. An essential part of the task of theology is to reflect dialectically on this historical process and on the political praxis of Christians within it.

We find the basis for just such dialectic reflection in Luther's work.

Models of Relationship of Church and State

In reinterpreting Luther's position, I would like to suggest several models of the relationship between church and state.

Separation of church and state In the first model, state and church are seen as separate powers, each in its own tightly defined sphere. Each has its own field of duties, completely separated from the other. The list of terms defining their separation can be extended indefinitely.

State	*Church*
secular	spiritual
social order	ecclesiastical order
public order	private order
body	soul
the power of the sword	the power of the Word
law	gospel
coercion	love
punishment	forgiveness

According to this model, the state is responsible for the secular order and the church for the spiritual order. Or the church is supposed to deal with its own internal organization, while the state regulates the society as a whole. The public order falls under the state's competence; the church sustains the private, intimate order. In simpler terms, the state takes care of the body, whereas the church nourishes the soul. The church uses the Word; the state, the sword. The church preaches the gospel; the state reinforces the law. The state monitors order and punishes delinquents; the church is the instrument of love and forgiveness.

This model of separation, often defended by Protestant churches or movements as well as by liberal, secular movements, can take two forms. Although they appear to exclude one another, they are based on the same premise: separation between church and state.

1. The first variant, the *demonization of politics*, makes the claim that everything belonging to the political sphere is fundamentally and existentially characteristic of the fallen world, an expression of human sin, or even the work of the devil. Politics is something dirty, and renewed Christians should not take any part in it. They already live in a regenerated world in the midst of the old and fallen one and consequently have "new life," which they might endanger by taking part in politics. So they confine themselves to the private sphere or to the company of the communion of the already redeemed. Persons or groups who hold this view demonize the political order, and consequently, the state, taking refuge in the spiritual order. They tolerate

the world because to live in it is inevitable, but they do so in expectation of heaven.

2. The second variant, the *autonomy of politics*, expresses an optimistic view of the state. The state is considered to be a part of God's creation, and thus, it is good. The same is true of the social and economic spheres. But even so, the competencies of church and state are separate. The church should never interfere with the realm of the state, according to this view. Politics, the economy, and society are each governed by laws proper to each. Each sphere has an inherent rationality whose rules our technical understanding should discover and apply. The church would pervert everything if it raised the questions that pertain to its own, spiritual order—such as the gospel, the will of God, and the spirit of Christ—in the order that is not within its competence. The church may talk about God, Jesus Christ, and the gospel in private, so to speak; it may awaken and strengthen personal morality, and promote unity in the family, but it should not tackle political, social, or economic questions. Those questions should be raised and responded to with technical reason. The church is not to infringe on the territory of these other, autonomous areas.

This second variant is especially attractive to Protestantism. These arguments were used—often by Lutherans—in a tragic attempt to legitimate Nazi ideology and the National Socialist system of Germany's Third Reich (1933 to 1945). This view is also widely held in the United States, it seems to me. There, the principle of separation of church and state became firmly established, permitting capitalism to develop on the basis of the legitimacy of its own rationality, and justified by the ideological approval of such a theological concept. Unfortunately, the separation of church and state, and of church and economy, has not kept North American missionary expansion from going on hand in hand with a technocratic, insensitive, and exploitative capitalism.

The two variants of the model predicated on separation of church and state both serve to legitimate the *status quo*. Although one of them demonizes and the other divinizes politics, both leave it untouched, either in its contingent, institutional forms or in the form of the rationale that informs it.

Alliance of church and state   This model can be schematized very simply:

church + state

The alliance model, like the above-mentioned separation model, predicates division into spheres of competence. Here, however, the separation is transformed into active, conscious, deliberate coopera-tion. The fields of action are divided, but both sides work together on a common project, for the sake of which the alliance was made.

In this model, two variants arise; when two bodies begin to co-operate, the question of how to divide the tasks—and the power—inevitably arises. Who shall decide over whom? Who shall have the power? In the final analysis, will the church dominate the state, or will the state dominate the church?

1. The first variant, the one in which *the church dominates the state*, is characterized by the authority of spiritual power over secular power. The state is submissive to the church, which wields both the sword and the Word, and the state complies with its task by delegation and commission from the church. This kind of relationship existed in certain periods during the Middle Ages. The best contemporary ex-ample of this model is found outside Christianity, in the control Shiite Islam exerts over the state and the political reality of Iran. The difficulty of finding similar examples in present-day Christianity suggests that the modern evolution of the state and the process of secularization either have led to the separation of the state and the church or have reversed the roles, making the church dependent on the state. Today, the state is the decisive power that either grants the church a specific but limited field of action, or employs it to strengthen its power and legitimate its ideology.

2. In the second variant of the alliance model, *the state dominates the church*. Two examples illustrate this variant. The first example emerges from Luther's time. Luther protested against the authority of the church over the state. Historical developments brought about the division of Christianity into two ecclesiastical bodies. The task of ref-ormation was carried out in Germany by the nobility and the princes, with Luther's encouragement and support. The establishment of ter-ritorial churches in which the religious affiliation of the citizens was determined by the choice of the ruler (the principle of *cuius regio, eius religio*), confiscation of ecclesiastical property, and even the ap-pointment of priests and bishops by the state—measures that Luther had meant to be only temporary—became all but permanent. In the Scandinavian countries, Lutheran state churches still exist.

The second illustration comes from Latin American history. The colonization of the continent was a joint project. State and church—the sword and the Word—formed an alliance in order to conquer the

"New World" and its indigenous population and to import black slaves. But the conquest was also understood as an expansion of Christendom. In this alliance, the state dominated the church. The model of "Christendom" merged economic and political colonization with the implantation of the Iberian culture and the Christian faith.

Both the model of separation and the model of alliance between church and state ultimately have the same result: both strengthen the interests of power. Whether the church serves the state directly; whether the church is confined to a private, spiritual sphere; or whether the state is granted complete autonomy, in all cases, the dominant interests are furthered.

To discover the principles that may guide the political action of Christians and Christian churches, we shall have to consider the question from another angle. The following question may help: Who is absent from the models presented so far? The people, for one. God, for another. In the foregoing models, institutions, the state, and the church and their relationship are dealt with, but neither the concrete needs of the people nor the will of God is mentioned.

The next model departs from just this point.

Church, state, and the struggle for justice   Here, Luther's position emerges. The relationship between church and state becomes more complex because both—as well as human beings—must seek their proper places in God's struggle against the idols, and on the side of the "planting" of the reign of God.[2]

Creation cannot be characterized as neutral territory. On the contrary, it is disputed; humanity lives in conflict. The ongoing battle is between God and the idols (in traditional language, the devil). This is not a Manichaean struggle, because the outcome is already known. God, who is greater than the idols, has gained the victory through the death and resurrection of Christ (*Christus victor*), by whom the idols

---

[2]This diagram is a modification of one elaborated by Ulrich Duchrow in his "Introduction" to *Lutheran Churches—Salt or Mirror of Society*, ed. Ulrich Duchrow (Geneva: Lutheran World Federation, 1977), 6–7.

GOD	CREATION/HUMANITY		IDOLS
Justice	New reality ✝ Old reality		Injustice
	(*Christus victor*)		
Truth	1. The human being		Lies
	(*simul justis et peccator*)		
Hope	Faith	Disbelief	Despair
	Hope	Despair	
Faith	Love	Selfishness	Sin
Conscience	2. The church		Alienation
	(word and sacrament)		
Love	Communion	Instrument of	Exploitation
	and liberation	domination	
Liberty			Oppression
Liberation	3. The state		Domination
	(coercive power, "sword," rationality)		
Fraternity	Defender of the	Instrument of	Egoism
	oppressed	the oppressors	
Equality	The common good	Domination of	Discrimination
		particular	
Resurrection		interests	Death
	Participative	Divided and	
	and equalitarian	discriminatory	
	society	society	

THE REIGN OF GOD → NEW HEAVEN AND NEW EARTH

(the devil) are subdued. The consummation will be the reign of God, the new heaven and the new earth.[3]

Nevertheless, for the time being, creation and humanity continue to be objects of struggle. There are many terms to characterize what is at stake; some of them appear in the columns on the left and the right. God defends justice against injustice, truth against lies, liberation

---

[3]Luther's terminology here is a heritage of an apocalyptic, Augustinian tradition. The distinction between "secular" and "spiritual," on the other hand, flows from the medieval debate about the "two swords." Luther placed this distinction within the more fundamental duality between God and the devil. (Cf. *Ulrich Duchrow, Christenheit und Weltverantwortung. Traditionsgeschichte und systematische Struktur der Zweireichelehre (Stuttgart: Ernstklett, 1970).*

against domination, and so on. History itself is the battlefield for this fight; humanity and creation are the objects of the dispute. But they are not merely spectators but participants. They may be instruments of oppression or of liberation. Faith centered in Jesus Christ, who is dead but risen, gives the certainty of victory even if, at the moment, this seems to be against all appearances.[4] Against the apparent victory of injustice, despair, oppression, and death, faith clings to reality and to God's promises, trusting in the power of justice, hope, liberation, and life.

The central column of the chart attempts to depict this conflict. History as a whole and the human being turn out to be the scene of the conflict between justice and injustice (in the chart called "new" and "old" reality). Our present reality is interpenetrated by the "old" and the "new," which are here terms of quality, not of chronology. "Old" is everything that in light of God's victory is doomed to disappear, even if it is now active and appears to be prevailing. "New" is everything that in light of the reign of God is destined to triumph, even if it seems very weak at present.

Frequently the dividing line between the "old" and the "new" passes through the midst of reality, the human being, the church, and the state. (On the chart, see the broken line.) As long as we still await the coming of God's realm in its fullness, no person, no institution, including the church, can claim to be totally "new." On the other hand, no one needs to despair in the face of the "old"; with Christ's advent, God's reign is already present, even though it continues to be contested by what has been overcome. At each step, we suffer the anguish of the "old" reality, even as we see signs of the "new."

The old and the new realities exist everywhere, overlapping and antagonistic. Any model of the relationship between church and state is too narrow if it is not set into the larger context of God's will and the world's conflictual reality. What is of interest is not the church-state relationship itself but how the cause of justice is faring. Without this overarching perspective, the issue of church-state relations degenerates into a technical distinction of realms, centered in the self-interests of the churches and states themselves. From the theological perspective here developed, however, church and state are measured by the extent to which they are found as being in service favoring human beings and peoples. This means: In evaluating persons and

---

[4]*LC*, Book of Concord, op. cit., 370.

institutions, including the church and the state, we must always ask ourselves whether they represent the "new" or the "old" reality, whether they favor justice or protect injustice.

Within this model, many variations are possible. It may be that both the church and the state are on the side of the "old" reality, forming a "holy" alliance as instruments of domination. Or the situation may be reversed; the church may be fundamentally an instrument of communion and liberation, whereas the state defends the oppressed and promotes a participative and egalitarian society. Because we are still on the way to the fullness of God's reign, this first possibility does not appear to be completely realized but always only approximately realized, requiring the permanent, critical vigilance of both the church and the state.

In a third possible variation, there may be a perverted state that acts as an instrument of domination, whereas the church serves Christ and thus critically resists the state. But the opposite is also possible. The church may continue to defend the old reality, seeking its own institutional preservation, built on privilege, whereas the state is the instrument of the people's wish for transformation and the construction of a just society. Usually, however, the relationship between church and state within the larger conflictive society is more complex. Ultimately, it is always a matter of discovering one's own place in the midst of God's fight against the idols and for the reign.

Criticism of Secular Power

The image of Luther as subservient to the political authorities is widespread. However, one can also find in his work harsh criticism against the princes. Luther's 1530 interpretation of Psalm 82 exemplifies his critique of secular power.[5]

Psalm 82

[1]God has taken his place in the divine council;
in the midst of the gods he holds judgment;
[2]"How long will you judge unjustly and show
partiality to the wicked?
[3]Give justice to the weak and the orphan;
maintain the right of the lowly and the destitute.

[5]LW 13:41–72, especially 41–61, 67–72.

⁴'Rescue the weak and the needy;
deliver them from the hand of the wicked."
⁵They have neither knowledge nor understanding,
they walk around in darkness;
all the foundations of the earth are shaken.
⁶I say, "You are gods,
children of the Most High, all of you;
⁷nevertheless, you shall die like mortals,
and fall like any prince."
⁸Rise up, O God, judge the earth;
for all the nations belong to you!

According to Luther, this is a political psalm. The first verse describes God as "standing up," that is, as a judge, in the midst of the congregation, to judge the "gods," that is, the political authorities, the princes. The judgment of them takes place from within the congregation; that is, the church transmits the judgment of the Word of God concerning the political authorities.

In his introduction, Luther shows how the princes, after having been liberated from the pope's tutelage through the Reformation's proclamation of the gospel, now want to be liberated from the gospel itself in order, in their turn, to become the dominators and even put themselves above God. They want to shut the mouths of the preachers who criticize them, Luther says, by accusing the preachers of being "seditious and rebels."[6] But the gospel is revolutionary, and it is part of the preacher's task to denounce what is evil.

Luther understands 82:2-4 as a description of the political office. Each ruler should have these verses written "in his room, over his bed, at his desk, and also on his clothes."[7] Luther distinguishes three tasks for each ruler: (1) to guarantee the free, critical, and prophetic preaching of the gospel; (2) to defend justice and the rights of the weak and abandoned; and (3) to guarantee the order, peace, and protection of the poor. The sequence of the tasks is not accidental. Free preaching comes first so that through its criticism, political power might be limited, contested in its claims to absoluteness, and reminded of its duties. Second comes the establishment of law and of justice as the basis for fulfilling the task of maintaining order, peace, and protection. All these tasks, according to the psalm, are not performed to

---

⁶LW 13:43.
⁷LW 13:51.

serve the interests of the powers that be, but always have the poor, the weak, the abandoned, the wronged, the oppressed, in mind.

According to Luther, the princes have seriously damaged their claims to authority by setting aside the gospel, putting themselves above God, governing for their own benefit, and oppressing the people. Therefore, the preacher must serve as the voice of God's judgment. Here, Luther criticizes the various kinds of preachers who try to avoid this responsibility: First, there are the unfaithful, lazy ones who, fearing punishment, prefer to keep silent and accommodate themselves. Second, the flatterers, who support the authorities out of self-interest and expedience. Finally, there are the slanderers, who prefer to criticize privately but do not have the courage to do so publicly in the worship service.

Against all these, Luther sets the true preacher, who does not defend his own interests and who does not compromise himself for fear of personal consequences or the persecution he may have to suffer. "So then, this first verse," Luther writes,

> teaches us that to rebuke rulers is not seditious, provided it is done in the way here described: namely, by the office to which God has committed that duty, and through God's Word, spoken publicly, boldly, and honestly. To rebuke rulers in this way is, on the contrary, a praiseworthy, noble, and rare virtue, and a particularly great service to God, as the Psalm here proves.[8]

There is no doubt about it: Luther cannot be said to legitimate either the total autonomy of politicians or the political passivity of the church.

The Church and Politics of Latin America

The dualist vision of the so-called doctrine of the "two kingdoms," separating the gospel and politics, church and state, cannot rightfully be ascribed to Luther. To be sure, he does distinguish their competencies and, in so doing, contributes to undoing the sovereignty of the church authorities over the political realm. The impact of Luther's contribution here was and still is profound.

[8]*LW* 13:50.

However, the situation of modern states is different from that in which the church claimed sovereignty over the political system, and more analogous to the situation described by Luther in his explanation to Psalm 82. Luther's admonitions about obedience to the secular authorities are of less immediate interest to us, whereas his call for criticism of and resistance to injustice and oppression gains relevance.

But let us consider the possible relevance of Luther's position in light of the contemporary political, economic, and social reality in Latin America, especially in light of the struggle for justice, against oppression. First, oppressive Latin American governments have been confronted frequently not only by the critical voice of the churches (to the degree that they have been true to their prophetic calling), but also by the power of organizations of poor people. The economic and political elites, even if they manage to hold onto a small part of society for themselves, must face growing movements of workers, rural laborers, civil servants, homeless people, street children, and so on, all of whom demand justice.

Second, in a period of transition from military to civilian governments, the churches have an opportunity to rediscover and renew their roots among the people and their historic task with the people. They may not need to continue to be the voice of the voiceless as they were during years of harsh repression. The churches are no longer the only place for popular organization that they once were in some Latin American countries. The question they face now is, Are they going to be satisfied to be an auxiliary voice of a people that is learning to speak its own language? For now, the churches can rejoice at the words of the people themselves, and re-echo them. Will they be content only to support those forms of organization the people are trying out in popular movements, labor unions, political parties, and so on? Or will the churches fear giving up control of these expressions of the popular struggle for liberation?

The question of whether the churches will be instrumentalized by other groups may be a real problem, and they have the right, like every other organized group, to be critical and watchful. However, the mark of the real church is not prudence but courage; not withdrawal behind one's own walls but mission; not accommodation with the mighty but solidarity with the oppressed. There will be reason for rejoicing if Christians and the churches do become an auxiliary voice instead of a voice speaking in the name of others; a channel through which the people can organize themselves instead of an organization that substitutes for the people.

Third, the churches have even less right to look to governing the people by dominating the state. Proposals that the churches patronize a political, social, and economic model of their own invention betray a longing for the bygone days of the church in power. The fundamental choice is not between church and state, spiritual or political power, but between justice and injustice, truth and lies, liberty and oppression, life and death. The gospel confronts both the church and the state with this option. The problem is not to defend the state from the interference of the church nor to protect the church from the control of the state; it is rather to participate in the struggle for justice and human rights, democracy and popular participation, whether it is in the order of the state or within the churches themselves.

Christians are never called to adapt to current political, social, and economic structures, whether they are the dualist variants of separation of church and state or models of coordination and alliance. The faith of Christians permits only a dialectic posture of distinction and critical participation, informed by the concrete circumstances of the current historic moment and guided by reasoned political practice. In some cases, *critical-constructive participation*[9] is legitimate, as when we have truly democratic and participatory political structures. Yet, these structures are less common than usually assumed. Many democratic countries, according to the constitution and the laws, are nevertheless heavily dominated by economic forces, increasingly of transnational dimension. Would a constructive participation, even if critical, be the most adequate relation? In the other extreme, we have seen cases in which the prevailing system is irremediably corrupted by injustice, oppression, and violence, without any realistic possibilities of fundamental change in sight. Here, a *critical-passive resistance* may be more appropriate, or it may be the only option left. Thus, for example, black slaves throughout the Americas have frequently resorted to forms of critical-passive resistance for centuries. This should not be misunderstood as a form of uncritical adaptation. Rather, through various practices—often their religious traditions—would allow them to preserve their ultimately free identity. Thus, they preserved their critical consciousness and the potentiality to struggle for freedom at a future time when new historic conditions would make it objectively feasible.

Finally, when spaces for a direct, transforming participation begin to open or have begun to be achieved—for example, when military

[9]This typology is taken from Duchrow, *Lutheran Churches—Salt or Mirror of Society*, 300–307.

dictatorships have to give way to civilian governments, as has happened in many Latin American countries in recent years—the politically conscious Christian chooses to engage in *critical-active transformation*. Two conditions call for this type of action: (1) the recognition of a fundamentally unjust system, characterized by social oppression; and (2) the existence of concrete possibilities of action, given by the historical process and the immediate circumstances. Presently, both these conditions exist in most Latin American countries.[10]

Supporting the organizations of the people, participating in them, and working toward the transformation of the established, oppressive system, is the political praxis, or action, that the will of God demands from Christians and their churches in most of Latin America today.

[10]In fact, there is always a period of transition in historical conditions. Thus, at the final stages of dictatorships, both objective and subjective conditions for a critical-active transformation develop. Thus, for example, mass street demonstrations in Latin America forced the transition from military dictatorships to elected civil governments, and in Eastern Europe, it was the same mass street demonstrations that forced the collapse of the Stalinistic bureaucratic regimes. This would not have been possible if there had not been previously the stage of critical-passive resistance with the potentiality to develop into an action of critical-active transformation.

7

Luther and the Issues

THE POLITICAL CALLING AND THE CHURCH

SELECTION

To the Christian Nobility of the German Nation Concerning the Reform of the Christian Estate (1520)[1]

The time for silence is past, and the time to speak has come, as Ecclesiastes says. I am carrying out our intention to put together a few points on the matter of the reform of the Christian estate, to be laid before the Christian nobility of the German nation, in the hope that God may help his church through the laity, since the clergy, to whom this task more properly belongs, have grown quite indifferent. (123)

The Romanists have very cleverly built three walls around themselves. Hitherto they have protected themselves by these walls in such a way that no one has been able to reform them. As a result, the whole of Christendom has fallen abominably.

---

[1]*LW* 44:123–217. Page numbers following the selections refer to this source.

In the first place, when pressed by the temporal power they have made decrees and declared that the temporal power had no jurisdiction over them, but that, on the contrary, the spiritual power is above the temporal. In the second place, when the attempt is made to reprove them with the Scriptures, they raise the objection that only the pope may interpret the Scriptures. In the third place, if threatened with a council, their story is that no one may summon a council but the pope.

In this way they have cunningly stolen our three rods from us, that they may go unpunished. They have ensconced themselves within the safe stronghold of these three walls so that they can practice all the knavery and wickedness which we see today. (126)

Let us begin by attacking the first wall. It is pure invention that pope, bishop, priests, and monks are called the spiritual estate while princes, lords, artisans, and farmers are called the temporal estate. This is indeed a piece of deceit and hypocrisy. Yet no one need be intimidated by it, and for this reason: all Christians are truly of the spiritual estate, and there is no difference among them except that of office. Paul says in I Corinthians 12 that we are all one body, yet every member has its own work by which it serves the others. This is because we all have one baptism, one gospel, one faith, and are all Christians alike; for baptism, gospel, and faith alone make us spiritual and a Christian people. (127)

The second wall is still more loosely built and less substantial. The Romanists want to be the only masters of Holy Scripture, although they never learn a thing from the Bible all their life long. They assume the sole authority for themselves, and, quite unashamed, they play about with words before our very eyes, trying to persuade us that the pope cannot err in matters of faith, regardless of whether he is righteous or wicked. Yet they cannot point to a single letter. (133)

Besides, if we are all priests, as was said above, and all have one faith, one gospel, one sacrament, why should we not also have the power to test and judge what is right or wrong in matters of faith? . . . We ought to march boldly forward and test all that they do, or leave undone, by our believing understanding of the Scriptures. We must compel the Romanists to follow not their own interpretation but the better one. (135)

The third wall falls of itself when the first two are down. When the pope acts contrary to the Scriptures, it is our duty to stand by the Scriptures, to reprove him and to constrain him, according to the word of Christ, Matthew 18, "If your brother sins against you, go and tell it to him, between you and him alone; if he does not listen to you, then take one or two others with you; if he does not listen to them, tell it to the church; if he does not listen to the church, consider him a heathen." Here every member is commanded to care for every other. How much more should we do this when the member that does evil is responsible for the government of the church, and by his evil-doing is the cause of much harm and offense to the rest! But if I am to accuse him before the church, I must naturally call the church together. (136)

CONTEXT

This treatise is one of the most important from 1520, a year during which Luther's relationship with the Catholic church became even more problematic and tense than it had been in 1517, the year in which he had posted the Ninety-five Theses.

The treatise has four basic objectives:

1. to appeal to the German nobility to act decisively against the misery prevailing all across Germany;
2. to denounce the exploitative activity of the church, activity he linked to the perpetuation of this misery;
3. to defend the cause of the Reformation, stripping the Roman church of its political authority; and
4. to discredit the ideology and theology that legitimated the church and its power even over secular authorities.

General Considerations

First, Luther calls on a specific group of persons—the Christian nobility—charging them to initiate the reforms he considers necessary in the church and in society. Luther sees in the German princes the class that has both the opportunity and the capability to act and to bring about what he calls "the reform of the Christian estate." "Estate" should be understood here not as a political institution but rather as a social situation.

Second, Luther underscores the competence of the German nobility to take on the necessary political tasks, and he does so at the expense of the political claims of the Roman church.

Third, in this treatise, Luther develops his doctrine of the priest-hood of all believers.

Fourth, Luther's criticisms of the pope's authority are much more radical here than they were in the Ninety-five Theses. Luther seems to have given up his earlier belief that the pope was unaware of the church's abuses in Germany. Here, the profile of Luther the reformer emerges clearly. He is not only a reformer of the church; he also advocates social and political reform.

Finally, the broad popular support this writing received, in part because of its rapid diffusion throughout Germany, shows once again that Luther was in an important sense giving voice to the hopes present in his time.

The Content of the Treatise

In the first part of the treatise Luther writes of three "walls" that sustain papal authority and protect the pope. Characterizing them as "walls of paper," he argues that their function is to preserve the power of the church structure.

The first "wall" is the thesis defended by the Roman church that ecclesiastical power is above secular power. This argument, Luther writes, justifies the pope's arrogating to himself supreme authority in both church and secular matters. Against this thesis, Luther holds that all Christians are members of the same body, the church. Although they may exercise different functions, all members have the same power. Distinctions among them are established not on the basis of power but on the basis of their functions as members of the same body.

Reflecting on I Corinthians 12, Luther distinguishes between secular power and ecclesiastical power. In some sense, this distinction is already available to Luther, in the medieval notion that the pope retains two swords, with jurisdiction in the ecclesiastical sphere and also in the political sphere. The pope's power to invest kings and emperors had provoked many conflicts during the Middle Ages. Luther elaborates the distinction between the "two swords" united in the power of the pope, and strips the pope of political power.

In this context, eminently political and at the same time theological, Luther develops his doctrine of the priesthood of all believers. He calls on the nobles, as baptized Christians and, therefore, priests of the body of Jesus Christ, to take up the task of stripping the institution of the church, or more precisely, the papacy, of its claims to jurisdiction in the political realm.

The other idea Luther develops in this context is that church authorities cannot survive independently. They are not self-sufficient but rather dependent—on the shoemaker, on the tailor, on artisans in general. Precisely for this reason, they cannot act as if they are superior to others. The notion of universal priesthood is underscored.

The second "wall" Luther identifies is the exclusiveness of ecclesiastical, principally papal, authority in the interpretation of the Bible. Luther argues that the notion of the exclusive papal authority to interpret Scripture is an ideological artifice designed to legitimate the political authority of the Roman church. The same person who holds the political power also holds the power to interpret Scripture; the clear implication is that no one can argue against church authority on the basis of Scripture.

Again, Luther responds with the theme of the priesthood of all believers. The Bible, he maintains, ought to be within reach of any Christian; any Christian has the right, even the duty, to argue using the Bible. The monopoly of biblical interpretation is a fable to maintain power. The keys to interpret the biblical text are given to all people. This he adduces using some biblical texts and even the Apostles' Creed. When we confess that "we believe in one holy church," he argues, "this is the object of faith and confession."

The third "wall" is the exclusive authority of the pope to call a council. The question arises, What recourse do we have in the face of ecclesiastical abuses or the exercise of arbitrary power? If the pope holds the monopoly on the interpretation of Scripture so that ecclesiastical authority cannot be argued against, then the only remaining route is to summon a council. But if only the pope has the authority to call a council, there are no roads left open. Luther argues here for the principle that any Christian can convene a council. However, he is realistic enough to know that in practice no Christian may do so. The princes, Luther believes, have both the right and the duty to call a council to bring about necessary changes in the church.

In a debate in 1519, Luther had discredited the idea that councils were infallible. Despite his earlier position, he now insists on the importance of a council, called this time by the princes, to bring about the reforms. He argues that, in Acts 15, it was not only St. Peter but the whole assembly of apostles that called the council in Jerusalem. Luther says he is part of a long conciliar tradition.

For Luther, the core of the problem is how to break the ideology that legitimates the ecclesiastical system. His treatise calls on those who are in a position to make changes to do just that.

Some Proposals for Reforming "the Christian Estate"

With respect to ecclesiastical reforms, Luther asserts that it is not up to the pope to name the bishops, because the pope is a foreign authority. He is in Rome, far from the problems of German national order. Luther suggests the creation of a national, German organization to name the bishops. This suggestion clearly indicates the radicality of Luther's proposal for reform.

In relation to the political order, Luther maintains that the pope's power is not greater than the emperor's. Imperial power does not belong to the pope. Addressing the fact that many German bishops are also princes, Luther proposes that political power ought to be independent in the application of civil law. Civil jurisprudence ought not to be left in the hands of church authorities. The church, he argues, ought not be able to inherit fiefs in those cases in which a feudal lord dies without an heir. Instead of being handed over to the church, the fief should go to the national political body.

Luther also suggests that the whole fiscal system of the Catholic church should be abolished. At the time, the church collected funds through many mechanisms: masses, feast days, funerals, indulgences, transfers of properties, and inheritance taxes. This was the foundation of the economic system that sustained the ecclesiastical system Luther sought to dismantle.

What place, what function, does Luther leave for the pope? The pope, Luther maintains, does not represent the heavenly Christ but the flesh and blood Jesus who preaches, suffers, and dies. Therefore, the pope should abandon all the ostentation of institutional power. As a representative of the divinity of Jesus, his only instrument should be the Word, the exhortation.

Luther also makes proposals for social reform. Trade, for example, should be diminished and agriculture encouraged, taking advantage of all idle land. This is a medieval element in Luther. He proposes the abolition of begging and criticizes the mendicant orders, advocating that they abandon their practice of begging and instead work to support themselves. He proposes replacing the works of Aristotle, basic to medieval scholastic theology, with the teaching of the Bible. He also proposes the creation of schools for women in every city. Other measures relate to prostitution. In fact, in this treatise his proposals for social reforms are numerous.

QUESTIONS AND REFLECTIONS

Our basic question is, What are the implications of Luther's appeal to the princes? Was this option the best one for the well-being of his people at that time? Or did he have other alternatives? Furthermore, how should we see this issue today, living in different settings and situations?

Luther's position on the relationship between the church and the political sphere had many consequences, among them some tragic ones. He added momentum to the development of absolutism in politics and to the development of absolutist states in assigning to the princes such an important role. He also does so in relation to the emergence of state churches, because he gives to the princes the responsibility to organize the church of the reformation. This was supposed to make way for a political structure more in keeping with his focus on the priesthood of all believers and his notion of the church as the people of God. In some treatises he delegates the task of organizing the Christian community to the congregation, to the community. But at the level of ecclesiastical organization, as he faces a series of practical problems, he appeals to the princes.

The dismantling of the old economic system provoked situations of great pauperization for the church of the Reformation. The princes, like any emerging political power attempting to strengthen itself, took advantage of this situation by confiscating formerly Roman Catholic properties, most often without rendering any social benefit.

Luther did not want to form another church, another denomination. He wanted the reformation of the church. Perhaps he asked himself, "Where to begin?" and he may have responded, "Where I live!" The German national elements one sees in the treatise are not absolutes but rather identify his social, political, and church context. But his hope is the reformation of all of Christianity, not only of his nation.

Whether Luther's decision in favor of the princes was strategic or tactical, it seems clear that in 1520 Luther was not aware of the distance and even the antagonism between the princes and the people. Ingenuously, he did not envision at that point the possibility that the princes

could be against the people. In some sense, in this treatise he is voicing
the historical grievances of the German nation, and he sees in the
princes, more by intuition than by an analysis of the reality, the possibility of making the proposed changes. Perhaps his error lay in not
being fully conscious of the potential danger in his proposal. The same
blindness reappears on the question of the church. Given the prevailing
political circumstances, Luther cedes to the princes the responsibility
to organize the church of the Reformation.

Later, he criticizes the princes sharply in treatises that are often
overlooked. At a particular juncture, for example, it becomes clear to
Luther that the princes are also oppressors and, Luther says, they are
even worse than the Turks, the world power that threatened the very
existence of the German nation. But in 1520, he was not aware of this
danger.

If we recall *The Magnificat*[2] (1521), we notice that Luther continues to think that the princes, as Christians, are equipped to carry
out the Reformation. But as baptized Christians, they should exercise
the political office in the way described in *The Magnificat*; that is,
they should exercise political power from the perspective of the humble, the poor, the weak. Again, Luther does not account for the possibility that those who hold power are ill-equipped to exercise it from
this perspective.

In our contemporary situations, we must go beyond the mere
transplantation of Luther's position to our context. We can take up
Luther's affirmation that political duties must be exercised by Christians on behalf of the well-being of the people. It is also worth noting
that political responsibility does require profound social reforms in
situations of injustice, exploitation, and oppression. In *The Magnificat*,
Luther stresses that political responsibility must be seen from the
perspective of the poor and weak, not of the wealthy and powerful—
a perception of great relevance not only for Latin America today but
even for most highly developed countries. It also applies to international economic relations.

But we cannot succumb to the temptation of simply appealing to
the conscience of those in political office that they take our good
advice. On the contrary, our contemporary democratic perception
makes us aware that political power must be exercised by the people
themselves. Taking into account the perspective of *The Magnificat*,

[2]*LW* 21:297–358.

we could say that it must be constituted from below. Political action will then be centered in those processes by which the poor and oppressed are strengthened to take upon themselves the political responsibility of shaping their own future. And in all this, we move beyond what Luther advocated in his time.

EDUCATION

SELECTION

To the Councilmen of All Cities in Germany That They Establish and Maintain Christian Schools (1524)[3]

First of all, we are today experiencing in all the German lands how schools are everywhere being left to go to wrack and ruin. The universities are growing weak, and monasteries are declining. . . . The carnal-minded masses are beginning to realize that they no longer have either the obligation or the opportunity to thrust their sons, daughters, and relatives into cloisters and foundations, and to turn them out of their own homes and property and establish them in others' property. For this reason no one is any longer willing to have his children get an education. "Why," they say, "should we bother to have them go to school if they are not to become priests, monks, or nuns? 'Twere better they should learn a livelihood to earn." (348)

Even though only a single boy could thereby be trained to become a real Christian, we ought properly to give a hundred gulden to this cause for every gulden we would give to fight the Turk, even if he were breathing down our necks. For one real Christian is better and can do more good than all the men on earth. (350)

A second consideration is, as St. Paul says in II Corinthians 6, that we should not accept the grace of God in vain and neglect the time of salvation. Almighty

[3]*LW* 45:347–78. The page numbers following the excerpts below refer to this citation.

God has indeed graciously visited us Germans and proclaimed a true year of jubilee. We have today the finest and most learned group of men. . . . (351)

Is it not evident that we are now able to prepare a boy in three years, so that at the age of fifteen or eighteen he will know more than all the universities and monasteries have known before? Indeed, what have men been learning till now in the universities and monasteries except to become asses, blockheads, and numbskulls? For twenty, even forty, years they pored over their books, and still failed to master either Latin or German, to say nothing of the scandalous and immoral life there in which many a fine young fellow was shamefully corrupted. (351–52)

The third consideration is by far the most important of all, namely, the command of God, who through Moses urges and enjoins parents so often to instruct their children. . . . (353)

. . . [E]ven if parents had the ability and desire to do it themselves, they have neither the time nor the opportunity for it, what with their other duties and the care of the household. Necessity compels us, therefore, to engage public schoolteachers for the children—unless each one were willing to engage his own private tutor. . . .

It therefore behooves the council and the authorities to devote the greatest care and attention to the young. Since the property, honor, and life of the whole city have been committed to their faithful keeping, they would be remiss in their duty before God and man if they did not seek its welfare and improvement day and night with all the means at their command. Now the welfare of a city does not consist solely in accumulating vast treasures, building mighty walls and magnificent buildings, and producing a goodly supply of guns and armor. Indeed, where such things are plentiful, and reckless fools get control of them, it is so much the worse and the city suffers even greater loss. A city's best and greatest welfare, safety, and strength consist rather in its having many able, learned, wise, honorable, and well-educated citizens. They can then readily gather, protect, and properly use treasure and all manner of property. (355–56)

Therefore, my beloved Germans, let us get our eyes open, thank God for this precious treasure, and guard it well, lest the devil vent his spite and it be taken away from us again. Although the gospel came and still comes to us through the Holy Spirit alone, we cannot deny that it came through the medium of languages, was spread abroad by that means, and must be preserved by the same means. For just when God wanted to spread the gospel throughout the world by means of the apostles he gave the tongues for that purpose. . . .

In proportion then as we value the gospel, let us zealously hold to the languages. For it was not without purpose that God caused his Scriptures to be set down in these two languages alone—the Old Testament in Hebrew, the New in Greek. (358–59)

Hence, it is inevitable that unless the languages remain, the gospel must finally perish. Experience, too, has proved this and still gives evidence of it. (360)

Now if (as we have assumed) there were no souls, and there were no need at all of schools and languages for the sake of the Scriptures and of God, this one consideration alone would be sufficient to justify the establishment every-where of the very best schools for both boys and girls, namely, that in order to maintain its temporal estate outwardly the world must have good and capable men and women, men able to rule well over land and people, women able to manage the household and train children and servants aright. (368)

By the grace of God it is now possible for children to study with pleasure and in play languages, or other arts, or history. Today, schools are not what they once were, a hell and purgatory in which we were tormented with *casualibus* and *temporalibus,* and yet learned less than nothing despite all the flogging, trembling, anguish, and misery. If we take so much time and trouble to teach children card-playing, singing, and dancing, why do we not take as much time to teach them reading and other disciplines while they are young and have the time, and are apt and eager to learn? For my part, if I had children and could manage it, I would have them study not only languages and history, but also singing and music together with the whole of mathematics. For what is all this but mere child's play? (369–70)

My idea is to have the boys attend such a school for one or two hours during the day, and spend the remainder of the time working at home, learning a trade, or doing whatever is expected of them. In this way, study and work will go hand-in-hand while the boys are young and able to do both. Otherwise, they spend at least ten times as much time anyway with their pea shooters, ballplaying, racing, and tussling. (370)

Finally, one thing more merits serious consideration by all those who earnestly desire to have such schools and languages established and maintained in Germany. It is this: no effort or expense should be spared to provide good libraries or book repositories, especially in the large cities which can well afford it. (373)

CONTEXT

Luther's first treatise on education, written in 1524 and excerpted here, is more programmatic, while the second, from 1530, contains essentially the same ideas but is a more occasional piece. After six years, some cities had already created schools, following Luther's proposals. The problem was then the resistance of parents to sending their children to these schools. The 1530 treatise, *A Sermon on Keeping Children in School*,[4] is an exhortation that they do so.

The Necessity for Educational Reform

The old medieval educational system was in crisis, reflecting the broader crisis of medieval society, which was in transition toward mercantile capitalism. The schools of the medieval system—those of the monasteries—pursued an Aristotelian-Thomistic educational philosophy and program, with opportunities for higher education limited to those who wished to pursue church careers. The fine reputation many of these religious schools had enjoyed had faded as they had stopped responding to the changing reality within which they functioned.

The Reformation had undermined economically and intellectually the foundations sustaining the medieval educational system. The political authorities had expropriated church properties. The religious career now demanded the personal sacrifice of those who wanted to pursue it. With regard to its content, the old system that had placed emphasis on the formation of priests but excluded training in preaching gave way to the new system, which focused precisely on preaching and the teaching of the Bible.

At the same time, the new socio-political and economic situation called for the creation of a new type of school. Individuals needed to be educated so that they could be deployed in commerce and public administration. The transition toward more centralized secular political structures required advisers and experts in administration and law.

[4]*LW* 46:213–58.

At the same time, trade was expanding and called for people skilled in this field.

Luther signaled the need for the educational system to broaden its scope to include the majority of the population. In this context, he spoke of the need for the citizens to finance the schools, arguing that they not only see the need for their own and their children's education, but also that they support the schools economically. If it is no longer necessary to spend money on indulgences, on buying relics, on pilgrimages, he asks, why not give this money—which would have been spent on superfluous things—on something as important as education instead? He goes so far as to contend that one should give one's whole fortune to sustain schools, because education is the most important activity.

The educational system must also be reformed, according to Luther, so that the "rediscovered" gospel not be lost again. Just because we have rediscovered the gospel does not mean that we have it forever; such a rediscovery, he argues, is like a quick rain that passes. We must work in order not to lose it. One of the devil's tasks is to persuade us that education is not important. Therefore, Luther admonishes, parents who do not want to send their children to school are being victimized by the devil, who in this way restricts the evangelical freedom they have received and experienced.

For Luther, a return to the old educational system, a retreat from the reforms that have already been implemented, is out of the question. He characterizes the old schools contemptuously as stables of asses and schools of the devil. That system cannot be reformed. There is only one alternative—to create a new one.

Education is a commandment of God, he argues, citing a whole range of biblical passages. God commands that we teach that schools are necessary. Again, the theological principle of the priesthood of all believers has implications for the social realm; in fact, it is the foundation for universal education. If all are priests, all ought to have access to the study of the biblical message of the good news of the gospel. The old school, which reached very few, should be replaced by a new school that reaches everyone.

The Agents of Educational Reform

Admonishing parents to send their children to school and calling on citizens to sustain the schools economically were not enough for Luther. Nor should the church be responsible. Educational reform is a political task. Whom should he exhort, then, to institute the schools? One might think he would call on the princes; he has accustomed us to this. Nonetheless, he does not do this. He knows that the princes have interests, concerns, and tasks on another level, and that they are not prepared to constitute schools everywhere. He proposes, therefore, that the municipal councils take up the task. He delegates the task of organizing the educational system to the state—not to the macro-state but to the local political institutions, the municipalities.

Several of Luther's suggestions are interesting because they help us see the significance he attributes to the educational task. He says, for example, that for every *gulden* that is invested in military expenditures 100 *guldens* should be invested in education. Imagine adopting such a formula today! Luther also asserts that the municipal authorities have the right, even the obligation, to require parents to send their children to school. He insists that schooling be universal and introduces the idea—never realized in his time—that education be obligatory.

The Church and the State as Beneficiaries of the New Education

A new educational system will bring benefits to both church and state. The benefits to the church are not obviously material benefits but rather benefits in relation to preaching. The church needs competent, prepared preachers so that that quick rain, that downpour of the gospel, will continue. Therefore, Luther emphasizes the preparation of pastors. He exhorts parents to send their children to school, not least of all in the hope that they will become pastors; for him there is no task more important than this one. Later, he adds that if one is not suited to preach the gospel, one can become a teacher, the second most important task. Finally he says that he does not know which of the two tasks is more important; possibly, the teaching vocation may be more important.

In the face of parental doubts about sending their children to be prepared as pastors, in the face of the possibility that there might later be no positions open, Luther reassures them by providing statistics of the parishes, the pastors, the sacristans needed to fill vacant posts. Moreover, he says, even if such fears were well founded—as in fact they were—they should trust in the promises of the Lord. It is necessary to take the risk, Luther insists; this is, after all, the task of the Christian, and no task is nobler than to preach the gospel.

At this point, Luther's pedagogic proposals are similar to those of the humanists. For example, he recommends the teaching of the ancient languages, Greek and Hebrew. For reasons different from those of the humanists, Luther believes that teaching the old languages provides direct access to the original text of the Bible, which he characterizes as better than the access mediated by a translation, whether in Latin or in German. The Bible is the most important book in the school, according to his proposals. Luther is clearly not thinking in terms of secular but of Christian schools, which is what he calls them.

Underscoring the necessity to study, Luther argues that the Holy Spirit is no fool. He also adds that history is one of the most important subjects for schooling. One learns from experience, he says, from the failures and the successes of the past. If we study history, we need not repeat everything from the start.

Schooling will also benefit the state, he writes. If the state builds schools for everyone, it will have better prepared citizens for all the tasks that need to be done in society, in addition to the public officials, men and women, whom the state needs. For tasks in public administration, the study of law was considered important. The study of medicine was included to meet the growing needs for health care. Later, he proposes that women prepare themselves to teach in the schools. Schools for boys and for girls should be separate, and women should teach in girls' schools. This, although we do not like it much, was very significant and a great advancement in that epoch. In medieval times, monasteries offered the only opportunities for formal education. Here, Luther is advocating universal education for both men and women.

Luther's Educational Proposals

With regard to methodology, Luther learns from the humanists. For example, he is opposed to the use of flogging, pressure on the students, punishment, and memorization. He advocates education that combines learning with playing. Children, he says explicitly, should learn playing, singing, and dancing.

His second proposal, perhaps more intuitive than analytic, is to link school and work; together with the common subjects, children should study a vocation or craft. Many parents did not want to send their children to school because they needed the income the children could provide by working. Luther's proposal to link basic education with daily life and even more with work responds to this concern.

He advocates the formation of good libraries and suggests some of the works that libraries should contain: (1) the Bible, (2) commentaries on the Bible, (3) languages, (4) history, (5) law, and (6) medicine. And, he maintains, libraries can dispense with the works of Aristotle!

QUESTIONS AND REFLECTIONS

For Luther, education is at the same time a secular and a religious task. He proposes the Christian school, not simply a school of the state, which is secularized. The teachers are not simply public officials; they exercise a spiritual function as well. Here, one can see with great clarity that, for Luther, the two realms are not separated into two static compartments.

In general, Luther embraces the humanists' principles of pedagogy and their emphasis on ancient languages. He does so principally because of his passion for the Bible and his interest in ensuring continuity in his evangelical discovery.

Luther's efforts had extraordinary historical influence in the arena of education, both within the Lutheran tradition and beyond it. Immigrant Lutheran churches that came to Latin America and to other continents carried with them this priority. When they planted roots, the construction of a school was generally their first common task. Only afterward was the church built. Often, the school also served as the place of worship.

Must we not raise the question as to whether in recent times, particularly in Third World countries, Protestantism has not contributed toward the development of a system of education for local elites without benefiting the impoverished masses of people? Could Luther's educational concepts have contributed toward this?

It is important to emphasize that Luther's historical moment and ours are distinct. This emphasis is important in order to defuse the criticism that Luther spoke prophetically but that the means he chose corrupted his "word." This would be true if we were to try to reproduce Luther's position today in our own reality. But we must take the historical and contextual differences into account. The question is, Who or what is the historical subject today? It is not the same subject as it was in Luther's time.

Luther's call to the municipal authorities and the new emerging bourgeoisie to take on the responsibility of education is a progressive move. Luther chose the correct actors in the historic moment in which he lived. Could he have chosen other ones? The peasants, for example, were hardly in a position to assume that important role. It could be argued that my position is the view of those who won. Since the peasants were later defeated, we can say that they were not in a position to be decisive historical subjects. We could argue that if Luther and others had not opposed the peasants, they might have had a chance.

But they probably did not. Whatever the historical speculation, the question of what our educational responsibility is today cannot be avoided. Can the impoverished be decisive actors in today's history? By "decisive actors" I would understand those social forces that can move history, the social structure, politics, to a new system, a new order that overcomes accumulation of wealth and the massification of poverty.

In Latin America, we have become accustomed to speaking of the importance of popular education, a kind of education that does not impose external contents, values, and patterns of living that alienate people. Rather, it builds on the capacity of poor and oppressed peoples to reflect on their own lives, come to a new awareness of the situation they live in, discover their own resources, and develop their potentialities. It is not geared principally to the training of individuals but rather to the strengthening of the community. We certainly must integrate these new perspectives into Luther's educational concerns.

THE ECONOMY AND THE COMMUNITY

SELECTION
_____

Trade and Usury (1524)[5]

I have been asked and urged to touch upon these financial evils and expose some of them so that, even though the majority may not wish to do right, at

_____

[5] *LW* 45:245–310.

least some people—however few they are—may be delivered from the gaping jaws of avarice. For it must be that among the merchants, as among other people, there are some who belong to Christ and would rather be poor with God than rich with the devil, as Psalm 37 says, "It is better for the righteous to have a little than to have the great possessions of the wicked." For their sake, then, we must speak out. (245–46)

At this point, therefore, I wish to tell of some of these tricks and evil practices which I have myself observed, and which good and pious people have described to me. This I do in order that one may realize how necessary it is that the rules and principles which I have set forth above be established and put into practice, if consciences are to be counseled and aided in matters of trade. . . .

. . . [T]here are some who have no conscientious scruples against selling their goods on time and credit for a higher price than if they were sold for cash. Indeed, there are some who will sell nothing for cash but everything on time, so they can make large profits on it. Observe that this way of dealing—which is grossly contrary to God's word, contrary to reason and every sense of justice, and springs from sheer wantonness and greed—is a sin against one's neighbor; for it does not consider his loss, but robs and steals from him that which is his. The seller is not trying to make a modest living, but to satisfy his lust for profits. According to divine law he should not sell his goods at a higher price on the time payment plan than for cash.

Again, there are some who sell their goods at a higher price than they command in the common market, or than is customary in the trade; they raise the price of their wares for no other reason than because they know that there is no more of that commodity in the country, or that the supply will shortly be exhausted, and people must have it. That is the rogue's eye of greed, which sees only the neighbor's need; not to relieve it, but to make the most of it and get rich at his expense. All such fellows are manifest thieves, robbers, and usurers. (261–62)

Some of them, when they see that they cannot otherwise effect their selfish profiteering transactions and establish their monopolies because others have the same goods and wares, proceed to sell their goods so dirt cheap that the others cannot meet the competition, and are forced either to withhold their goods from sale, or to face ruin by selling them as cheaply as their competitors do. Thus, the greedy ones get their monopoly after all. Such fellows are not worthy to be called human beings or to live among men; they are not even worth admonishing or instructing, for their envy and greed is so open and shameless that even at the cost of their own losses they cause loss to others, in order that they may have the whole place to themselves. The temporal authorities would do right if they took from such fellows everything they had, and drove them out of the country. It would scarcely have been necessary to tell of such practices, but I wanted to include them so that one might see what great villainy there is in trade and commerce, and to make evident to everyone what is going on in the world, in order that everyone may know how to protect himself against such a dangerous class. (264–65)

How could it ever be right and according to God's will that a man in such a short time should grow so rich that he could buy out kings and emperors? They have brought things to such a pass that everybody else has to do business at the risk of loss, winning this year and losing next year, while they themselves can always win, making up their losses by increased profits. It is no wonder that they quickly appropriate the wealth of the whole world, for a pfennig that is permanent and sure is better than a gulden that is temporary and uncertain. But these companies are always dealing with permanent and sure gulden for our temporary and uncertain pfennigs. Is it any wonder that they become kings and we beggars? . . .

    . . . This is why no one need ask how he may with a good conscience be a member of a trading company. My only advice is this: Get out; they will not change. If the trading companies are to stay, right and honesty must perish; if right and honesty are to stay, the trading companies must perish. The bed is too narrow, says Isaiah, one must fall out, the covering is too small, it will not cover both [Isa. 28:20]. (271–72)

SELECTION

Fraternal Agreement on the Common Chest of the Entire Assembly at Leisnig (1523)[6]

Property, resources, and receipts for the common chest   In order that our Christian faith—in which all the temporal and eternal blessings won by our Lord and Savior Christ out of pure grace and mercy are granted unto us by the eternal God—may bear fruit in brotherly love, and this love truly express itself in deeds of tender kindness, we, the aforesaid general parish assembly, acting unanimously, for ourselves and our posterity have ordained, established, and set up a common chest, and by these presents we do now ordain, establish,

[6]*LW* 45:176–94. Luther wrote a preface for this document.

and set up this same chest on the authority of this our fraternal agreement as to purpose, scope, and form, as follows. . . . (178–79)

Disbursements and assistance from the common chest   We, the members of this parish and our posterity, therefore solemnly purpose and promise henceforth to provide food, sustenance, and support through our ten elected directors out of our common chest, to the limit of our resources as God grants us grace, and as occasion demands to make the following disbursements, namely:

> Disbursements for the pastoral office
> Disbursements for the office of sacristan
> Disbursements for the schools
> Disbursements for the poor who are aged and infirm
> Disbursements for the support of orphans and dependent children
> Disbursements for home relief
> Disbursements for the relief of newcomers from without
> Disbursements for the maintenance and construction of buildings
> Disbursements for the purchase of grain for the common stores.
>   (186–91)

CONTEXT

In 1520, Luther had written a sermon having to do with the practice of usury. In 1524, he picks up the theme again in *Trade and Usury*, which is published in the context of a Germany in economic transition, characterized by increased reliance on money, on the development of trade, the growth of cities, and diversification.

There are already some indications that confrontation with the peasants will occur. Luther's tone in the treatise is pessimistic, especially at the end. He wonders whether he will manage to convince one single person of his case. Evil is so strong that God will surely have to exercise justice by other means. Luther may be glimpsing the following year's upheaval. Perhaps this treatise is an effort to prevent the worst.

His interest in writing *Trade and Usury* is to call attention to the unjust behavior of the merchants. He tells about the difficulties some persons have confessed to having encountered in trying to be good Christians and also tradespeople. Luther writes the tract for them, for those who would rather "be poor with God than rich with the devil."

Setting Prices

Luther's principal criticism is aimed at the prices of commodities, which were established by the merchant. He argues that it should not be this way. Prices ought not to be subject to what we would today call the law of supply and demand; they should be fixed, Luther says, in accord with the needs of the populace. He denounces the manipulation of prices by those who sell only in their own interest. And he asserts that the true purpose of selling is to satisfy a real need.

Luther recognizes that commercial exploitation grows in proportion to the need; the greater the need for the product, the higher the price. Merchants who sell products that become scarce in the market raise the price because the demand is larger than the supply. Such merchants are taking advantage of a situation of need. Under such conditions, commerce is nothing more than simple robbery. Luther uses this word repeatedly. The greater the need, the more expensive the product becomes. The neighbor's need is the motive for robbery.

Luther writes:

Among themselves the merchants have a common rule which is their chief maxim and the basis of all their sharp practices, where they say: "I may sell my goods as dear as I can." They think this is their right. Thus occasion is given for avarice, and every window and door to hell is opened. What else does it mean but this: I care nothing about my neighbor; so long as I have my profit and satisfy my greed, of what concern is it to me if it injures my neighbor in ten ways at once? There you see how shamelessly this maxim flies squarely in the face not only of Christian love but also of natural law. How can there be anything good then in trade? How can it be without sin when such injustice is the chief maxim and rule of the whole business? On such a basis trade can be nothing but robbing and stealing the property of others.

When once the rogue's eye and greedy belly of a merchant find that people must have his wares, or that the buyer is poor and needs them, he takes advantage of him and raises the price. He considers not the value of the goods, or what his own efforts and risk have deserved, but only the other man's want and need. He notes it not that he may relieve it but that he may use it to his own advantage by raising the price of his goods, which he would not have raised if it had not been for his neighbor's need. Because of his avarice, therefore, the goods must be priced as much higher as the greater need of the other fellow will allow, so that the neighbor's need becomes as it were the measure of the goods' worth and value. Tell me, isn't that an un-Christian and inhuman thing to do? Isn't that equivalent to selling a poor man his own need in the same transaction?

When he has to buy his wares at a higher price because of his need, that is the same as having to buy his own need; for what is sold to him is not simply the wares as they are, but the wares plus the fact that he must have them. Observe that this and like abominations are the inevitable consequence when the rule is that I may sell my goods as dear as I can.[7]

Luther rejects this formula. But then, How to fix the price of a commodity? Luther offers some guidelines. The point of departure ought to be what the day laborer earns or receives for his or her day's work in making the commodity. It should also include an appraisal of risk, the cost of manufacturing and shipping, and the purchase of raw materials. The price of the commodity, determined on the basis of these data, would not be altered despite heavier demand or diminished production.

"The rule ought to be," Luther writes,

not, "I may sell my wares as dear as I can or will," but "I may sell my wares as dear as I ought, or as is right and fair." For your selling ought not to be an act that is entirely within your own power and discretion, without law or limit, as though you were a god and beholden to no one. Because your selling is an act performed toward your neighbor, it should rather be so governed by law and conscience that you do it without harm and injury to him, your concern being directed more toward doing him no injury than toward gaining profit for yourself. But where are there such merchants? How few merchants there would be, and how trade would decline, if they were to amend this evil rule and put things on a fair and Christian basis![8]

Luther certainly recognizes the need for trade; he sees that the bartering of goods is not enough. In this sense, his vision accounts for the emerging economic reality. It also introduces criteria regarding what is worth trading. He is opposed, at this point, to the purchase of goods that can be dispensed with, such as the spices and silk from Asia that were being introduced into Germany at the time. These were, Luther believed, luxurious, superfluous commodities. Here he reveals a nationalist bent. Trade ought to be limited to those things that are really necessary and produced in one's own country.

[7]*LW* 45:247–48.
[8]Ibid., 248–49.

Usury and Christian Trade Practices

Not without some irony, Luther maintains that there are four ways in which a Christian merchant can deal with the neighbor:

(1) *Allowing Others to Take or Steal Our Goods*. Luther acknowledges that this attitude has little appeal among tradespeople. Still, to tolerate the taking of our goods would be one Christian way of working with the neighbor, according to the Sermon on the Mount.

(2) *Giving Freely to Everyone What They Need*. This would be the ideal. Luther concedes difficulties if this were put into practice. There would be few merchants.

(3) *Lending Out Our Goods, Recovering Them When and if They Are Returned, Counting Them as Losses if They Are Not Returned*. Loans would be granted only to those really in need. In this case, we should be prepared to make loans even when we know it cannot be recouped. No guarantees of repayment should be required in advance. Whoever lends for profit or more is a "notorious and damned usurer," Luther writes.

Luther makes it clear that he believes his proposals could be adopted only by Christians and among Christians, and not in society as a whole. Since everyone would rather receive than lend, the state should become involved so that abuses are avoided. Those who can repay what they have received as loans, should do so. Luther also suggests that the lender not lend what is really necessary to support the lender's family, children, and servants. This is to avoid finding oneself in the situation of needing to require the immediate repayment of a loan, in order to avoid pressuring the neighbor. If one lends, one should lend what one is ready and able to lend.

(4) *Buying and Selling for Cash or Paying in Kind*. Demonstrating some awareness of economic cause and effect, Luther concludes that

> if there were no such thing in this world as becoming surety, if the free lending portrayed in the gospel were the general practice, and if only hard cash or wares on hand were exchanged in trade, then the greatest and most harmful dangers and faults and failings of trade and commerce would be well out of the way. It would then be easy to engage in all sorts of business enterprises, and the other sinful faults of trade could the more readily be prevented. If there were none of this becoming surety and this lending without risk, many a man would have to maintain his humble status and be content with a modest living who now aspires day and night to reach an exalted position, relying on borrowing and standing surety. That is why everyone now wants to be a merchant and get rich. From

this stem the countless dangerous and wicked devices and dirty tricks that have today become a joke among the merchants. There are so many of them that I have given up the hope that trade can be entirely corrected; it is so overburdened with all sorts of wickedness and deception that in the long run it will not be able to sustain itself, but will have to collapse inwardly of its own weight.

In what has been said I have wished to give a bit of warning and instruction to everyone about this great, filthy, widespread business of trade and commerce. If we were to tolerate and accept the principle that everyone may sell his wares as dear as he can, approving the practice of borrowing and forced lending and standing surety, and yet try to advise and teach men how to act the part of Christians and keep a good and clear conscience in the matter, that would be the same as trying to teach men how wrong could be right and bad good, how one could at the same time live and act in accordance with divine Scripture and contrary to divine Scripture. These three errors—that everyone may sell what is his as dear as he will, also borrowing and becoming surety—these are like three fountainheads from which the whole stream of abomination, injustice, low cunning, and trickery flows far and wide. To try to stem the flood without stopping up the source is a waste of effort and energy.[9]

Later, Luther will denounce actual trade practices. But he does see some structural causes in the standards that seem to prevail in the economic order.

Merchants' "Lies and Tricks"

Luther does not mince words in condemning commercial practices he believes are wrong. Selling on credit at a higher price than for cash, he says, is robbery. He also denounces merchants who acquire a monopoly of a certain article, allowing them to fix their own price. He condemns cases in which merchants with greater financial power sell the same article as other merchants, but below cost to break the latter and gain monopoly. Or cases in which buyers take advantage of a certain merchant who needs quick cash, buying the product from that merchant for less than its value, only because the seller is in dire economic straits. With his usual bluntness, Luther calls those who do these things murderers and stranglers.

Other targets of his criticism are cases in which, foreseeing that an article will be needed more than it is at present, several merchants

---

[9]Ibid., 260–61.

create a monopoly together and corner the product in order to sell it for a greater price later. He denounces cases of financial pressure, even among merchants themselves, for example, in not paying up a credit that one could pay. He opposes charging interest, supporting his position even with biblical quotations.

The merchants complained about the highway robbers, who in fact were a problem at the time. Luther argues that this is a minor problem compared with the continuous robbery practiced by the merchants themselves. The merchants who rob all the time, he writes, complain about the thieves who rob occasionally.

Luther condemns the large companies that were beginning to be organized on the basis of diversified production. They are instruments of the most powerful kind of pressure, he argues, pressure that is used to break small merchants and producers. Such large companies sell some products below cost in order to gain a monopoly and recoup the difference by overcharging on another product. The proprietors of these companies become more powerful than kings and convert the population into beggars.

The Trade System

In large part, the treatise is addressed to the consciences of those merchants who want to be good Christian merchants. Luther suggests what is permissible and what is not. A Christian may not remain in a monopolistic company, for example; the only alternative is to leave, because it is not possible to behave in a Christian manner in such companies.

But Luther also sees that it is not possible to approach the matter simply by admonishing people's consciences. Regulation by the state is also necessary, principally in the areas of setting prices and controlling commodities. Furthermore, he says—despite the fact that he sees how the princes punish the small thieves while the big thieves are their friends—the state and the princes ought to curb exploitation.

An Alternative: The Communal Chest

The communal chest is an attempt to seek viable economic alternatives at the local level, inspired by another, more community-minded ethical perspective.

The necessities were very acute, especially for pastors, teachers, older people, those who were ill, widows, and the destitute. All those who had left the monasteries and convents because of the Reformation were cast into poverty. Luther suggests that properties owned by the Roman church be confiscated for the community's use. Many princes took advantage of this practice simply to add to their own real estate. But Luther's idea was that they be destined for the use of the community, that they support economically those persons who had left the monasteries as well as those who had decided to remain in them.

The communal chest was also meant to sustain the new church economically and to assist in the creation of schools. In some places—in Wittenberg, for example—this system worked for some time. A clause in its bylaws specified that only the unemployed of Wittenberg, and not of other cities, would receive economic assistance from the communal chest. The clause was necessary because people in need from other localities were being sent to Wittenberg, where they asked for and received support.

Although Luther inspired the creation of the communal chest, he was not the author of the regulations in the Leisnig document quoted earlier. When the town of Leisnig organized its own treasury, it sent him the regulations and asked for his opinion. Luther provided a short introduction or preface supporting the regulations.

The regulations foresee three assemblies a year and the annual election of members of an executive committee for the chest, composed of two merchants, two artisans, three peasants, and two representatives of the municipal government. There is also a provision that when there is an abundant harvest, a part of it will be left for times of bad harvest; this was an attempt to keep prices from fluctuating.

In the Leisnig community, the chest did not function for long. It failed because the municipal authorities, who represented the interests of the bourgeoisie, stopped supporting the chest financially.

QUESTIONS AND REFLECTIONS

A first question we might raise in assessing Luther's economic stance is related to Luther's own class position and what impact this might have had on his economic views. We know that his father was a former peasant who managed to ascend the social ladder, becoming an entrepreneur in mining. He had nurtured dreams of further social ascendancy for his son Martin.

In entering the monastery, Luther dispelled his father's dreams, indicating that social ascendancy was no longer one of his own ideals. By contemporary standards, we would probably describe Luther's lifestyle as middle class. He lived neither in luxury nor in poverty. In later years, his wife would complain often about the hardships of running a large household, often with many guests and limited resources. While no one in his time sold as many books as Luther did, he never received any money for any of his works.

Luther's economic writings reveal a deep compassion for the poor. His denunciations of economic abuses reveal a strong concern and commitment to justice. His economic views are radically centered in the basic needs of the people, not in profit making. In fact, he saw a permanent conflict between these two.

The Reformation movement was, at least until 1525 and to some degree even after, a popular movement. The people, including the peasants, identified with Luther's thought and his aims, and they treated him as a respected authority. In 1525, when circumstances obliged Luther to take an option he had originally wanted to avoid, his popularity and that of the Reformation suffered profound damage. However, even after the Peasants War, the Reformation persisted, at least in part, as a popular movement. But its historical success or failure then depended on the policies of the princes. Could economic justice be expected from them?

This leads us to a second question: To what degree are Luther's analysis and proposals accurate and workable? And, is there a sense of the structural dimensions of economic exploitation or does Luther expect to contribute to better economic relations by addressing the consciences of individuals?

In the treatise on *Trade and Usury*, ethics and exhortation on the individual level predominate, whether addressed to the tradespeople or to the princes. That there is also some consciousness of the structural problems as well as of the relation of the princes to the emerging large companies is significant for its time. Luther sees a certain connection between the princes and the wealthy merchants. He says the big thieves are killing the small ones. In this sense, the recommendation that the princes regulate economic activity is ingenuous and mistaken. Perhaps it is grounded in Luther's fear of social disorder that might put the religious Reformation in danger; perhaps his apocalyptic vision influenced his thinking in the sociopolitical sphere. Today, it is clear we cannot share or accept this perspective.

We must recognize that Luther's critique is better elaborated than his proposals. To some extent, he resists making proposals, despite having formulated a few. For his denunciation, Luther received high praise from Karl Marx, who declared that Luther was one of history's greatest economists. Perhaps we should be a bit more reticent.

Luther's proposals are a good deal less creative; for the most part, they are suggestions that continue to presuppose the medieval system. His position on usury, for example, reiterates criticisms common in the Middle Ages, an indication perhaps that he did not see the significance of the accumulation of capital for the emergence of the new economic system. So his suggestions here tend to be naive. Luther had trouble perceiving the structural links between the emerging political power and the economic power. The proposal that the state control the economic activity might seem salvageable, but insofar as this power to control is delegated to the princes, who were closely related to the most economically powerful merchants, it is corrupted. The viability of Luther's proposal remains dependent on the good will of these same people.

The communal chest was a more promising approach than the call to the princes, possibly because it called for action at a local level, where there was the potential to develop some alternative. But in general, Luther did not recognize that trade and finance were mobilizing the economic development in his age. He believed that trade could be regulated by returning to medieval ideas, that is, his proposals do not advance beyond capitalism but rather represent a return to the Middle Ages.

In any case, we can be proud of his harsh criticisms—even on a moral level—of the merchants, and of his solidarity with those who had to pay the price of the process, the exploited ones. His proposals, nevertheless, run against the movement of the historical process. We are inspired by his prophetic voice but we are left with the enormous task of building an economic system centered on the people's basic needs.

WAR

Whether Soldiers, Too, Can Be Saved (1526)[10]

What men write about war, saying that it is a great plague, is all true. But they should also consider how great the plague is that war prevents. If people were good and wanted to keep peace, war would be the greatest plague on earth. But what are you going to do about the fact that people will not keep the peace, but rob, steal, kill, outrage women and children, and take away property and honor? The small lack of peace called war or the sword must set a limit to this universal, worldwide lack of peace which would destroy everyone.

This is why God honors the sword so highly that he says that he himself has instituted it (Rom. 13:1) and does not want men to say or think that they have invented it or instituted it. For the hand that wields this sword and kills with it is not man's hand, but God's; and it is not man, but God, who hangs, tortures, beheads, kills, and fights. All these are God's works and judgments. (96)

The office of the sword is in itself right and is a divine and useful ordinance, which God does not want us to despise, but to fear, honor, and obey, under penalty of punishment, as St. Paul says in Romans 13 [:1–5]. For God has established two kinds of government among men. The one is spiritual; it has no sword, but it has the word, by means of which men are to become good and righteous, so that with this righteousness they may attain eternal life. He administers this righteousness through the word, which he has committed to the preachers. The other kind is worldly government, which works through the sword so that those who do not want to be good and righteous to eternal life may be forced to become good and righteous in the eyes of the world. And although God will not reward this kind of righteousness with eternal life, nonetheless, he still wishes peace to be maintained among men and rewards them with temporal blessings. He gives rulers much more property, honor, and power than he gives to others so that they may serve him by administering this temporal righteousness. Thus God himself is the founder, lord, master, protector, and rewarder of both kinds of righteousness. There is no human ordinance or authority in either, but each is a divine thing entirely. (99–100)

---

[10]*LW* 46:93–137.

No war is just, even if it is a war between equals, unless one has such a good reason for fighting and such a good conscience that he can say, "My neighbor compels and forces me to fight, though I would rather avoid it." In that case, it can be called not only war, but lawful self-defense. . . . (120)

The third question is whether overlords have the right to go to war with their subjects. We have, indeed, heard above that subjects are to be obedient and are even to suffer wrong from their tyrants. Thus, if things go well, the rulers have nothing to do with their subjects except to cultivate fairness, righteousness, and judgment. However, if the subjects rise up and rebel, as the peasants did recently, then it is right and proper to fight against them. That, too, is what a prince should do to his nobles and an emperor to his princes if they are rebellious and start a war. . . . For God has appointed subjects to care for themselves as individuals, and has taken the sword from them, and has put it into the hands of another. If they rebel against this, get others to join them and break loose, and take the sword, then before God they are worthy of condemnation and death. (125, 126)

"Suppose my lord were wrong in going to war." I reply: If you know for sure that he is wrong, then you should fear God rather than men, Acts 4 [5:29], and you should neither fight nor serve, for you cannot have a good conscience before God. (130)

SELECTION

Army Sermon against the Turks (1529)[11]

For the Scriptures prophesy to us about two cruel tyrants who, before the last days, will devastate and destroy Christendom, one spiritually, with cunning or false worship and doctrine against the true Christian faith and the Gospel. . . . That is the pope with his papacy, of which we have written enough elsewhere.

The other will do it with the sword, physically and externally, in the most horrible way. Daniel prophesies this categorically in Chapter 7 [:25], and Christ, in Matthew 24 [:21], speaks of a tribulation without equal on the earth. This is the Turk. Given then, the imminent end of the world, it is necessary that the

---

[11]*WA* 30/2, 160–197 [*Heerpredigt wider den Türken*]. On the same subject, see *LW* 46:161–205. [Selections from *Army Sermon against the Turks* translated from German into English by translator.]

devil attack Christendom beforehand with all his power in the most terrible way, giving us the truly mortal blow, before we rise up to heaven.

Whoever wants to be a Christian in these times, should fix his heart on Christ and think no more of peace and good days. The hour of this tribulation and prophesy is at hand. At the same time, our trust and comfort in the coming of Christ and our redemption are not far from us, either, but rather they will follow immediately, as we will soon hear. Wherefore persevere and be assured that the Turk is surely the last great rage of the devil against Christ, with which he will reach his limit and pour out all his fury against the kingdom of Christ. Beyond that, he is the greatest punishment of God upon the earth against the thankless and godless detractors and persecutors of Christ and his Word, and is without doubt the harbinger of hell and of the eternal punishment. For Daniel says that, after the Turks, will follow rapidly the judgment and hell. (162)

It is sufficient for them that they are Christians and saints of God through Christ our Lord, as Daniel says. . . . This is not to say that they should throw away their weapons and shields and defenselessly let the Turks kill them, as the martyrs outside of war have done, which they still do and still should do. But rather because Christians are subject in body and goods to worldly authority, and all of them, having been called each one by his respective authority to fight against the Turks, should act as faithful and obedient subjects—which they surely do if they are Christians—using physical force with gusto, striking, killing, destroying, and bringing about all possible damage with complete confidence as long as they are able to move a muscle. For this is what their secular authority is ordering them to do, and that to which they owe obedience and service, which is what God wants of them, even unto death, see Romans 13 [1], and Titus [1]. (179)

CONTEXT

Army Sermon against the Turks

The situation to which *Army Sermon against the Turks* responds is very clear. At the moment of its writing, the Turks were laying siege to Vienna and threatening to take all of Europe. At the moment of its publication, the resistance had lifted the Turkish siege of Vienna. But while he was writing it, Luther thought that Vienna was falling and the threat to Europe was dramatic and real.

Luther's tract has a strong apocalyptic tone, which does not appear as clearly in his other writings. It is important to look at this dimension in Luther. Here, he describes an imminent end and exhorts to decisive action because of the proximity of this end.

The sermon contains an allegorical interpretation of the book of Daniel. Luther, confronting a concrete situation, believes he can discover in the text of Daniel the elements to interpret the historical situation in which he is living. He distinguishes between two tyrants, one spiritual—the pope—and the other terrestrial—the Turk. This is a tyrant at the service of the devil, but the devil is finally at the service of God's purposes. The devil advances against Christ and punishes impious Christians for their faithlessness. In this combat against Christ, there will be many martyrs.

The question here is whether or not this serves a divine purpose. If this is somehow part of God's plan, is there any sense in struggling against it? Perhaps one should submit and suffer. Luther contends instead that acquiescing in this kind of suffering is an attitude to take when one wants to make holy war, an idea Luther always resisted. Holy wars, he claimed, were organized by the pope with the help of emperors and kings against the Turks. For Luther, the war against the Turks was a political activity in defense of the people, in which all Christians, even women and children, should participate.

Luther's treatise has three purposes. In the first place, he wished to cheer his German compatriots in the face of war. The war against the Turks, he says, ought not to be undertaken under the name of Christendom, nor should it be waged as a battle against enemies of the Christians. The war should be fought beneath the secular flag. The army should call itself imperial, not Christian. Even though Christians will be protected by the angels, even though Christ's grace is sufficient, still they should not throw down their weapons. When faced with the option of counseling ethical passivity, Luther insists that grace does not limit participation. Grace leads into the struggle, he declares. (At the same time, the fact of grace does set limits on doing all possible damage to the enemy.)

Then Luther issues a call to repentance. Christians should repent, for war with the Turks is a punishment for Christian faithlessness.

Finally, Luther exhorts his compatriots to risk both body and goods. He is thankful for the time of peace that has gone before, but he counsels that this is now a time of war and total mobilization is necessary. Those who will be captured should remain faithful to the Christian faith. In other matters, they should obey their new lords, except if the Mohammedans would oblige them to fight against Christians. In this case, they should choose death instead.

Whether Soldiers, Too, Can Be Saved

This treatise, written in 1526, one year after the war against the peasants, reflects among other things on the question of whether it is permissible to wage a war of subversion against those in political power.

Luther begins by discussing the vocation of waging war, which he says is an honorable vocation. What is important, he says, is to know when to go to war. War is a "plague" and should be undertaken only when its aim is clear and just, when the struggle is against injustice and to prevent a greater evil.

He distinguishes among three types of war. The first is the war that subjects undertake against their superiors. This is not permitted, despite the fact that in some paragraphs Luther leaves the door open a crack. In an historical overview he shows that this type of war is one way in which God punishes bad rulers. Subjects ought not to rebel unless their ruler is both a tyrant and a lunatic.

The second type is the war between equals, between kings. Here, Luther does not legitimate the war of conquest but rather the war of defense. The just war is the defensive war. He says that one should not participate in an unjust war even if not doing so costs one's life. The Crusades, for example, are not just wars. God does not want war to be made for the sake of the faith; rather, God wants the Word to be preached. In this case one should not participate either, but rather disobey to the last. If the war is defensive, on the other hand, and if one cannot prove that the war is unjust, one should participate, even risking losing one's life.

The third kind is the war of superiors against subjects. This is the experience that had been lived through in the year before the treatise was written. Luther is persuaded of the right of the superior to make war against an uprising, as if it were a war of defense. If there are unjust governors who do not promote peace, still it is preferable to endure injustice than to promote insurrection.

For Luther, war is a secular activity that has to do with our social organization, with the necessary protection of persons and their lives. He rejects holy war as a means to promote the faith and he does not believe one should call a war holy that is undertaken to defend the social order. At the same time, he is opposed to pacifism, because war is a constant possibility in the secular arena.

QUESTIONS AND REFLECTIONS

A first question would focus on whether an apocalyptic vision like Luther's ends in an ethical passivity or whether it represents, on the contrary, a more intense motivation to act. This is precisely the theme of the apocalyptic in the Bible and in history. Here a point of commonality between Luther and Thomas Müntzer. Müntzer also has this vision, which drives him to struggle with such determination. The apocalyptic vision does not carry with it as a logical or ethical consequence the lack of motivation to act. Rather, it expresses a lived dialectic.

A second question relates to the concepts of holy war and secular war. One of the keys to understanding Luther is that he does not make separations but distinctions; nor does he make identifications. If we read Luther's texts applying the concept of separations or identifications we will not do justice to Luther's thought.

A secularized war, in the sense that it has nothing to do with faith, does not exist for Luther. Nor is there any such thing as a neutral or secularized profession; this is what we see when we study the theme of *Beruf*. So, too, the profession of soldier is holy. Everything that a Christian does should be holy, for he or she always does everything as a Christian.

But to make war to spread the gospel or to defend the faith is something else. Here Luther feels obliged to make the distinction that the legitimate purpose of war is to defend life, goods, and nation. One participates in war as a Christian, and in this it is holy. This is a dialectic of distinction but not of separation. Luther did not argue that war is totally secularized in the sense that it has nothing to do with faith, with a Christian's beliefs, with God's will, and with the Bible. The same notion applies to the professions, politics, economics, education, the home, and so on.

A third question is whether we can trace parallels between Luther's situation and ours. For example, which are the powers that threaten us today? We cannot accept Luther's hierarchical perspective, that what is above is basically the good and what comes from below is the evil. According to this principle, uprising is not licit but repression is. In the structures that prevailed in the Southern Cone until recently, with military dictatorships, we were confronted with the evil of repression. The threat does not come from those who organize and attempt to produce changes but rather from those who maintain the structures of power against the people. In our countries the doctrine of national security has been an instrument that in our countries used to justify the domination of our peoples. This is why we should struggle against it. There is no alternative for Christians but to struggle for human rights and for justice.

That Luther can reconcile the concept of authority with the principle of disobedience of the soldier if the war is not just shows, fortunately, that Luther's concept of authority is not absolute, but rather open to new situations and perspectives.

In an attempt briefly to systematize our observations, we might highlight the following points:

1. The desacralization of war was a positive advance in Luther's time.

2. In good measure, Luther is in agreement with changes such as the professionalization of the army that occurred as a result of the transition from feudalism to the modern age.

3. The idea of the just war comes from the Middle Ages. Luther adopts this position because it restricts the possibility of war and limits the participation of Christians in it. That is, he suggests conditions for participation. He does not believe that a Christian should participate in a given war simply because the rulers order it.

4. There are evident transformations in the nature and the scope of war, difficulties in determining whether a war is just or not. Everyone will say that the war begun by others is aggressive and that theirs is defensive. It is practically impossible to determine when war is just or unjust.

5. Our commitment to peace must be much more radical than Luther's. Although he imposed some limitations on war, although he said that war is a plague, Luther also declared that, in particular situations, it was a lesser evil to avoid a greater evil. Our commitment to peace must be immediate. The Lutheran churches should move closer to the churches of the pacifist tradition, such as the Mennonites and the Quakers. Luther's criticism of pacifists was in large measure unjust, even in his own time; so was his call for the repression of pacifists.

6. The commitment to justice and law, the struggle for peace, according to Luther, are the part of the purview and content of the political task. In this respect, there is a point of convergence between Luther and ourselves.

7. Today we no longer assign the task of the defense of rights and the promotion of justice only to those who govern, as Luther did. For us, today, it is a task for the whole people. All pacifist movements must be valued. In this way the search for peace becomes real.

8. In light of the devastating effects of today's sophisticated weapons and warfare, it becomes imperative that we abolish, politically and juridically, the institution of war as a solution to international political conflicts.

RESISTANCE AND VIOLENCE

SELECTION

Admonition to Peace, A Reply to the Twelve Articles of the Peasants in Swabia (1525)[12]

We have no one on earth to thank for this disastrous rebellion, except you princes and lords, and especially you blind bishops and mad priests and monks, whose hearts are hardened, even to the present day. You do not cease to rant and rave against the holy gospel, even though you know that it is true and that you cannot refute it. In addition, as temporal rulers you do nothing but cheat and rob the people so that you may lead a life of luxury and extravagance. The poor common people cannot bear it any longer. The sword is already at your throats, but you think that you sit so firm in the saddle that no one can unhorse you. This false security and stubborn perversity will break your necks, as you will discover. (19)

The peasants have just published twelve articles, some of which are so fair and just as to take away your reputation in the eyes of God and the world and fulfill what the Psalm [107:40] says about God pouring contempt upon princes. Nevertheless, almost all of the articles are framed in their own interest and for their own good, though not for their best good. . . .

[12]*LW* 46:17–43.

In the first article they ask the right to hear the gospel and choose their pastors. You cannot reject this request with any show of right, even though this article does indeed make some selfish demands, for they allege that these pastors are to be supported by the tithes, and these do not belong to the peasants. Nevertheless, the basic sense of the article is that the preaching of the gospel should be permitted, and no ruler can or ought to oppose this. Indeed, no ruler ought to prevent anyone from teaching or believing what he pleases, whether it is the gospel or lies. It is enough if he prevents the teaching of sedition and rebellion. (22)

[To the peasants:] . . . [I]t is easy to prove that you are taking God's name in vain and putting it to shame; nor is there any doubt that you will, in the end, encounter all misfortune, unless God is not true. For here is God's word, spoken through the mouth of Christ, "All who take the sword will perish by the sword" [Matt. 26:52]. That means nothing else than that no one, by his own violence, shall arrogate authority to himself; but as Paul says, "Let every person be subject to the governing authorities with fear and reverence" [Rom. 13:1].

How can you get around these passages and laws of God when you boast that you are acting according to divine law, and yet take the sword in your own hands, and revolt against "the governing authorities that are instituted by God"? Do you think that Paul's judgment in Romans 13 [:2] will not strike you, "He who resists the authorities will incur judgment"? You take God's name in vain when you pretend to be seeking divine right, and under the pretense of his name work contrary to divine right. Be careful, dear sirs. It will not turn out that way in the end. (24–25)

. . . [E]ven a child can understand that the Christian law tells us not to strive against injustice, not to grasp the sword, not to protect ourselves, not to avenge ourselves, but to give up life and property, and let whoever takes it have it. We have all we need in our Lord, who will not leave us, as he has promised [Heb. 13:5]. Suffering! suffering! Cross! cross! This and nothing else is the Christian law! But now you are fighting for temporal goods and will not let the coat go after the cloak, but want to recover the cloak. How then will you die and give up your life, or love your enemies and do good to them? O worthless Christians! Dear friends, Christians are not so commonplace that so many can assemble in one group. A Christian is a rare bird! Would to God that the majority of us were good, pious heathen, who kept the natural law, not to mention the Christian law! (29)

Now, dear sirs, there is nothing Christian on either side and nothing Christian is at issue between you; both lords and peasants are discussing questions of justice and injustice in heathen, or worldly, terms. Furthermore, both parties are acting against God and are under his wrath, as you have heard. For God's sake, then, take my advice! Take a hold of these matters properly, with justice and not with force or violence and do not start endless bloodshed in Germany. For because both of you are wrong, and both of you want to avenge and defend yourselves, both of you will destroy yourselves and God will use one rascal to flog another. (40–41)

SELECTION

Against the Robbing and Murdering Hordes of Peasants (1525)[13]

In my earlier book on this matter, I did not venture to judge the peasants, since they had offered to be corrected and to be instructed; and Christ in Matthew 7 [:1] commands us not to judge. But before I could even inspect the situation, they forgot their promise and violently took matters into their own hands and are robbing and raging like mad dogs. All this now makes it clear that they were trying to deceive us and that the assertions they made in their *Twelve Articles* were nothing but lies presented under the name of the gospel. To put it briefly, they are doing the devil's work. This is particularly the work of that archdevil who rules at Mühlhausen,[14] and does nothing except stir up robbery, murder, and bloodshed; as Christ describes him in John 8 [:44], "He was a murderer from the beginning." Since these peasants and wretched people have now let themselves be misled and are acting differently than they promised, I, too, must write differently of them than I have written, and begin by setting their sin before them, as God commands Isaiah [58:1] and Ezekiel [2:7], on the chance that some of them may see themselves for what they are. Then I must instruct the rulers how they are to conduct themselves in these circumstances. (49)

The peasants have taken upon themselves the burden of three terrible sins against God and man; by this they have abundantly merited death in body and soul. In the first place, they have sworn to be true and faithful, submissive and obedient, to their rulers. . . . Since they are now deliberately and violently breaking this oath of obedience and setting themselves in opposition to their masters, they have forfeited body and soul. . . .

[13]*LW* 46:45–55.
[14]Thomas Müntzer [—Trans.]

In the second place, they are starting a rebellion, and are violently robbing and plundering monasteries and castles that are not theirs; by this they have doubly deserved death in body and soul as highwaymen and murderers. . . .

In the third place, they cloak this terrible and horrible sin with the gospel, call themselves "Christian brethren," take oaths and submit to them, and compel people to go along with them in these abominations. Thus they become the worst blasphemers of God and slanderers of his holy name. Under the outward appearance of the gospel, they honor and serve the devil, thus deserving death in body and soul ten times over. (50–51)

For in this case a prince and lord must remember that according to Romans 13 [:4] he is God's minister and the servant of his wrath and that the sword has been given to him to use against such people. If he does not fulfill the duties of his office by punishing some and protecting others, he commits as great a sin before God as when someone who has not been given the sword commits murder. If he is able to punish and does not do it—even though he would have had to kill someone or shed blood—he becomes guilty of all the murder and evil that these people commit. For by deliberately disregarding God's command, he permits such rascals to go about their wicked business, even though he was able to prevent it and it was his duty to do so. This is not a time to sleep. And there is no place for patience or mercy. This is the time of the sword, not the day of grace. (52–53)

Therefore, dear lords, here is a place where you can release, rescue, help. Have mercy on these poor people! Let whoever can stab, smite, slay. If you die in doing it, good for you! . . . If anyone thinks this is too harsh, let him remember that rebellion is intolerable and that the destruction of the world is to be expected every hour. (54, 55)

CONTEXT

Do Christians have the right or even the duty to resist constituted authorities? What would be legitimate means, and what would be illegitimate means, for necessary resistance?

To re-examine Luther's position on this question is difficult, given his alliance with the princes during the Peasants' War. Although there are still some who defend his position, even those who in other respects admire him express at least embarrassment regarding this chapter of his life and work.

The writings on which we focus in this section cover a very short but decisive span of time in Luther's activity: from February/April 1525 to July of the same year. Many Luther scholars maintain that in these months a parting of the waters occurs in Luther's life. Up until this point, the argument goes, the Reformation movement had been popular, whereas afterward at least the Lutheran Reformation lost its support among the people. There is a good deal of truth in this point of view, but it is too simplistic.

The economic, social, and political changes associated with the historical transition from feudalism to incipient mercantile capitalism profoundly affected the living conditions of the peasants, who comprised about three quarters of the German population of about fifteen million. Both the civil rights and the civil obligations of the peasants were affected; the old German law was being replaced by Roman law.

In the feudal order, the peasants lived in servitude. Their living conditions were clearly difficult; they were obliged to work and to give lifelong obedience to their respective feudal lords. At the same time, they were assured of certain rights, among them the right to live and to support their families on land assigned to them, access to enough produce for family consumption, and access to hunting and fishing.

Large-scale changes in the social and economic orders—among them the replacement of the barter system by a monetary economy, the growth of the cities, the creation of new, independent professions in the artisan sector, the expansion of the mining sector, the strengthening of centralized state structures under the aegis of territorial princes—had direct and indirect repercussions on the lives of the peasants. Centralization, for example, brought with it greater financial obligations, so taxes and tributes were increased and rights and exemptions were restricted.

The feudal lords—a class in decline—transferred to the peasants the new commitments that had been imposed on them and doubled those commitments. The system of servitude entered into crisis, creating some breaches favorable to the peasants. Some serfs were able to become small farmers, producing for the cities. Others were freed or fled to the cities, where they became artisans. The majority of the peasant population, however, continued to suffer a steady curtailment of their civil rights.

In this context, peasants' uprisings occurred with increasing frequency. In Germany, there were significant rebellions in 1492, 1502, 1513, and 1517, before the large-scale Peasants' War of 1524 to 1525.

Among the many documents articulating their claims one is of particular importance: the *Twelve Articles of the Peasants of Swabia*, written in February of 1525. The peasants' demands include: (1) the right to elect pastors; (2) abolition of the "small tithe" (of vegetables), but not of the "large tithe" (of cereals); (3) liberation from servitude (because all were redeemed by Christ); (4) freedom to hunt and fish; (5) the right to chop wood in the forest for domestic consumption; (6) recompense for compulsory labor; (7) pay for extra work for the lord; (8) reduction of rents; (9) elimination of arbitrary punishments; (10) restitution for pastures and fields taken from the commons; (11) abolition of inheritance taxes that burdened widows and orphans; and (12) examination of these demands in light of Scripture.

These claims were not of a piece; on the contrary, they reflect the complexity of the peasant movement and, therefore, the diversity of its claims. Some demands—for example, the end of servitude—required fundamental changes in the prevailing order. Others asked only for relief from certain living conditions—as, for example, the end of arbitrary punishment. Finally, others aimed only at reestablishing medieval rights that had not been respected, like the right to hunt and fish freely. The influence of the Reformation and of Luther in particular is clearly detectable, for example, in items 1, 3, and 12. Luther, together with the elector Prince Frederick of Saxony, is mentioned by the peasants themselves as a possible negotiator in this situation.

Luther's Response

On April 19, 1525, Luther writes his *Admonition to Peace: A Reply to the Twelve Articles of the Peasants of Swabia*. His objective is clear, in the title and throughout the work: He wishes to exhort to peace and understanding between the parties. He confirms his opposition to the peasants' insurrection, which he had already expressed in 1522. He is convinced that insurrection is never justified, no matter how good the cause that motivates it, because in an insurrection, irrational values prevail that make it impossible to establish justice.

Even so, Luther in no way justifies the princes. On the contrary, he directs himself to them first and forcefully, accusing them of being responsible for injustices that have become intolerable. Even God is against them, he says, and could raise up peasants from among the stones! The princes are exercising unjust and unbearable tyranny. For this reason, they themselves—the princes—are responsible for the unrest in the countryside, and not he, Luther. (Note here Luther's self-defense in the face of accusations that he is ultimately responsible for the peasants' unrest.) Luther goes on to exhort the princes to enter into agreements with the peasants, to lower taxes, and to alleviate the situation. He tries to show that there would be indirect advantages for the princes themselves: They would have nothing to lose, whereas the use of force against the peasants would carry risks with it.

Then Luther turns to the peasants. The crux of this argument is that any peasant movement will be compromised if it interprets itself in the name of Christ. In the name of Christ, in fact, the Christian has only one right: that of suffering violence but never of perpetrating it. Redeemed by Christ, Christians remain servants.

Using another line of reasoning, however, Luther shows himself open to the peasants' claims. They should use human and natural law, not divine law, Luther contends, to make their claims. Here, he can support them. On this point Luther clearly distinguishes (but does not separate) the spiritual and the secular orders. He fears that the peasant movement is identifying the two orders in the same way that medieval Catholicism did, with such unhappy consequences.

At the end of the treatise, Luther urges the disputing parties to come to an agreement. In the end, when the treatise is published, the revolt has already exploded in various parts of Germany. Luther decides to travel through Thuringia, advising and trying to convince the peasants not to use violence. He does not understand the historical process unfolding so rapidly, and remains convinced of the deceitfulness of the peasants who, even when they call on him to arbitrate, do not await his response. He watches as irrationality prevails.

Feeling betrayed, he believes that the time has come for the princes to reestablish order, and so on May 6, 1525, he produces the sadly celebrated treatise *Against the Robbing and Murdering Hordes of Peasants.* Here, he indicts the peasants on the following counts: (1) They have broken their oaths of obedience to the authorities; (2) they have become thieves and murderers; and (3) they have tried to cover up their crimes with the name of Christ.

Directing himself to the princes, Luther then exhorts them to forget their reticence and to employ their power to reestablish and maintain order. He admonishes them to suffocate the rebellion with all the resources at their disposal. Blessed are those, he fulminates, who in this task stab, wound, and kill seditious peasants like rabid dogs! His last sentence illustrates his full intentionality: "If anyone thinks this is too harsh, let him remember that rebellion is intolerable and that the destruction of the world is to be expected every hour."[15]

Once again, events overtook Luther. When the treatise appeared, the war was already over, the peasants had been decimated, and Thomas Müntzer was dead. The decisive battle took place in Frankenhausen on May 14, 1525. Approximately 6000 peasants died. Poorly armed themselves, they faced soldiers armed by the princes. Among the soldiers, there were only six casualties. Müntzer fled, but he was captured, tortured, and beheaded. The princes seized their victory as an occasion to extend the massacre. In these circumstances Luther's treatise was published; it was then seen as a theological justification for the repression and bloodbath already in process.

The princes felt legitimated, the peasants betrayed, and even Luther's closest friends could not hide their disillusionment and their shock. In July of 1525, Luther wrote his *Open Letter on the Harsh Book against the Peasants*.[16] In spite of everything, Luther ratified his earlier positions. He remained convinced that the rebellion had had to be put down. He only recalls having said too that, once the rebellion was over, the princes should exercise mercy toward the innocent and the guilty alike. Once the peasants had been defeated, it would not be fair to call on him to justify continuing the repression.

QUESTIONS AND REFLECTIONS

A first set of questions might be: Did Luther have a static vision of society? Did he oppose structural change? Important structural changes were occurring during his epoch. His call to the German nobility against the tutelage of the pope was already a call for structural change. Perhaps he did not favor all the changes that should have been made in his time, but he did favor very radical structural changes in Germany.

The ascent of the bourgeoisie, the incipience of absolutism, the transition from feudalism to the first forms of mercantile capitalism— all of these were profound historical changes. In general, Luther did not attempt to impede them; on the contrary, he became a spokesperson for some of them. At the outset he was even a leading figure

[15]*LW* 46:55.
[16]*LW* 46:63–85.

in change. It is true that sometimes we can observe—in his vision of commerce, for example—medieval values or concepts. This only shows that the issue is too complex simply to say that Luther did not favor structural change and that he often proposed palliative solutions.

A different question is whether he sacrificed social reform for religious reform. Certainly Luther's priority was to maintain the evangelical freedom the Reformation movement had discovered. This was more important than whatever social reform was sought. When he had to decide between the two kinds of reforms, he was undoubtedly inclined to maintain and proceed with religious reform. It is highly likely that his belief that the rediscovery of the gospel could be lost again in the midst of chaos deeply influenced the stances Luther took in the Peasants' War.

On the other hand, we should not be tempted to overestimate Luther's influence on the historical events. Sometimes the episode is presented as if he had been the cause and as if he could determine the outcome. Luther tried to intervene, but on both sides events had already occurred. Luther's treatise *Against the Robbing and Murdering Hordes of Peasants* came out when the peasants had already been defeated; it did influence the behavior of the princes, in that it legitimated their decision to massacre the peasants after they had already been defeated. However, it was not in itself a decisive element in the defeat of the peasants.

More significant for us is the following question: Was Luther consistently and always against all forms of resistance from below? We must challenge the assumption that underlies this question.

Luther had already opted for the support of the princes in 1520 when he wrote *To the Nobility of the German Nation Concerning the Reform of the Christian Estate.*[17] At this historical moment there was a sort of national unity and consensus around Luther's cause. He could count on the support of all social sectors, even the peasants. He enjoyed such popularity among the peasants that in 1525 they considered him a possible arbiter in the conflict. But even from this first moment, there was for Luther a tie to and a choice for the princes, in awareness of the historical role they played. Luther's loyalty deepened after 1521, when he came under the protection of the elector Frederick the Wise.

Certainly, Luther also saw society as hierarchically structured. In this, he was rather medieval. In any case, Luther remains faithful to

[17]*LW* 44:123–217.

this option from the start. When the peasants' issue comes to a head, he attempts to negotiate; however, when the inevitable explosion occurs, he calls on the princes to put an end to the whole mess. He never regretted this. In later texts he declared it necessary.

After the annihilation of the peasants, there are occasions on which Luther expresses more openness on the issue of resistance and violence. He articulates, for example, many and sharp protests against the political and economic tyranny of the pope, the bishops, and the clergy. In this, he is not completely consistent; one would expect him to remain faithful to his hierarchical perspective. But his attitude is one of disobedience. Here, he calls on the princes so that with the support of a large national movement, they can break the connection with these foreign, ecclesiastical authorities.

In other texts, Luther entertains the possibility that subordinate authorities rise up against superior authorities in cases in which the law has been broken. The issue of whether or not the princes could rise up against the emperor was a very difficult one. Although in many texts Luther says that the emperor is owed obedience because he is the emperor, even though he is not supporting the evangelical cause, Luther eventually concludes that the princes may rise up against the emperor.

There are even texts, principally from the 1530s, in which Luther says it is legitimate for authorities of the state apparatus to revolt against the prince. Here, his prime interest is in the preservation of his basic evangelical discovery. The fact is that this is a break with his earlier contributions in the sense of simply obeying the superior authorities. He urges disobedience and resistance when the faith is not respected. There are also texts in which he recommends disobedience when the second table of the Decalogue, concerning the social and political realm, is not fulfilled. For example, disobedience is licit and even obligatory when the war is unjust.

With regard to the means of resistance, there are many texts in which Luther sees the Word as a means of resistance, and he backs this with biblical texts—Acts 5:29, for example: "We must obey God rather than any human authority." There are places where Luther argues that the rulers and the theologians are those most easily captivated by Satan. The good ruler is a rare bird, he says often; for this reason they should be criticized on the basis of the law. Resistance by means of the Word, by means of testimony, is not only permitted but required.

Then we can find in Luther some elements that are essential in the struggle of active, nonviolent resistance: the principles of law and justice; the disposition to suffer rather than make others suffer; the refusal to deny the possible conversion of the oppressor in the face of criticism and the disposition to suffer, and by these means to unmask and disarm the oppressor. Is the principle of active, nonviolent resistance a general principle in Luther? In Luther, we do not find general or absolute principles; the contradictions have shown this.

At another point, Luther says that it is all right to use violent methods, although this does not become an absolute principle, which is applicable in all situations. Here, one of Luther's statements from the 1530s is apt: "If a tyrant attacks and persecutes one subject, he attacks and persecutes all the rest as well, one after another; from that would follow that if one allowed that to happen, he would disrupt, devastate, and destroy the whole regiment and realm."[18]

Or on another occasion, Luther wrote: "So one is more obligated and indebted to obey rights and laws than [to obey] a tyrant. . . . If he were to take by force from one man his wife, from another his daughter, from a third his lands and goods, and the citizens and subjects got together, and could not tolerate his violence and tyranny any longer; they would be within their rights to kill him, as they would any murderer or highwayman."[19]

We conclude that Luther had a fundamentally hierarchical view of society, a heritage from medieval times. He did break with the tutelage of the church over the political realm, a significant and liberating contribution to his time. But he left the basic hierarchical structure of society as a whole unchallenged. Hence, his frequent stress on obedience toward the authorities and his aversion to insurrection.

In the episode of the Peasants' War, he believed the very cause of the gospel was being threatened. His evangelical concerns and his hierarchical view of society combined to compel him to oppose the peasants in their revolt and to encourage the princes violently to crush them.

It was not a stance to be proud of; on the contrary, it is one to be ashamed of. At the same time, once the hierarchical view of society has been challenged and a radically democratic perspective has replaced it, a wholly new approach can flourish.

[18]From *Dr. Martin Luthers sämtliche Werke,* Vol. 62 (Frankfurt-Erlangen, 1854), 190; quoted in *Widerstand gegen die Staatsgewalt. Dokumente der Jahrtausende,* edited by Fritz Bauer (Frankfurt/Hamburg, 1965), 97. [English translation by translator.]

[19]Ibid., 98. [English translation by translator.]

The intense solidarity Luther showed with people in need, in terms of economic issues, for example, can then bear fruit also in the political realm. It is significant that even Luther himself could open cracks in the monolith of authority and obedience. Further work on these perspectives remains as our theological task. We are Christians who live in other times and contexts and with new awareness of the social and political structures prevailing in today's world. We do not restrict ourselves to repeating Luther's words but endeavor to produce a creative reconstruction of his basic assumptions and discoveries.

8

Luther's Legacy

Luther lived in a turbulent epoch; dramatic transformations were occurring in culture, in economy, in the social and political orders, in
religion, and in morality. Luther never enjoyed the privilege nor suffered the disgrace of reflecting on the convulsive historical process
from a distance. Forced to think, speak, and act from the center of
events—events that seemed to swoop down on him—he managed to
maintain a peculiar freedom of conviction and action. Much of what
he said and did was in response to events that demanded he take a
position. His concern was not, nor could it be, an ahistorical coherence.

In many ways, Luther was a human being well matched to his
turbulent epoch. We should remember not only the young Augustinian
monk, with his questions about a merciful God and about his own
salvation. We must also recall the later Luther, with his frequent and
intense personal tribulations. One of his most significant contributions
was to have reflected theologically on this personal reality, which
also—and perhaps especially—characterizes the believer, and to have
coined formulations of such theological precision and faith to describe
them: *simul justus et peccator*, for example.

Like very few other historical personages, Luther lends himself to
a host of divergent images. Seventeenth-century Lutheran orthodoxy
saw in him a "prophet," the stubborn and unbendable defender of
purest doctrine. Pietism saw in Luther the "convert," who through
faith and the Bible found peace with God. The Enlightenment celebrated Luther as the "liberator from narrow-mindedness"[1] that the

---

[1]Franz Lau, *Luther,* translated by Robert H. Fischer (Philadelphia: Westminster
Press, 1963), 13.

doctrinal authoritarianism of the church generated. Pan-Germanists lauded Luther as a "national German hero." More recently, the psychiatrist Erik H. Erikson attempted to explain Luther on the basis of his relationship with his father.[2] And post-Tridentine Catholicism came to see in Luther the very incarnation of the devil.[3]

In some of these characterizations, the apologetic interest is all too clear; in others, a particular universe of values. All of them, however, have in large or small measure some legitimate point of reference in the life and work of Luther.

But how to assess Luther? We cannot elude the question. On the one hand, Luther remains alive and present today not only because we form part of his theological and historical legacy but also because there is so much of him even today that also underlies other churches and the modern world as a whole.[4] In the last one hundred years a prodigious effort has been made to rediscover Luther. Publication of the monumental Weimar edition of Luther's writings began in 1883; since then, more than 100 volumes have been published. These texts have formed the basis for what came to be called a Luther renaissance.

A century of research seems to have established consensus on at least some dimensions of Luther's life and work. Yet, even these points must become matters of consciousness in our contemporary reflection on Luther. The question, How to assess Luther? can and should be approached self-consciously and contextually. What do we bring in, with, and under our intent to assess this man and his work?

Luther himself was characteristically "offensive," that is, unconcerned with the preservation of traditions, concerned rather to proclaim the gospel without fear, always challenging new situations. For this reason, the study of Luther is especially—and perhaps only—relevant to the extent that it asks what help (or impediment) Luther

---

[2] Erik H. Erikson, *Young Man Luther: A Study in Psychoanalysis and History* (New York: Norton, 1958).

[3] See Harding Meyer, "Lutero na opinião da Igreja Católica Apostólica Romana," in *Estudos Teológicos* I (1961): 3–28; Paul Schempp, "Der Mensch Luther als theologisches Problem," in *Gesammelte Aufsätze* (Munich: Christian Kaiser Verlag, 1960), 258–95, especially 265–77; Hans Joachim Iwand, "Luthers Theologie," in *Nachgelassene Werke*, Vol. 5 (Munich, 1974), 52–60; Erwin Iserloh and Harding Meyer, *Lutero e luteranismo hoje* (Petrópolis: 1969), 7–19, 85–102.

[4] Otto Hermann Pesch, a Catholic theologian, speaks of his anonymous presence as "Junker Jörg" (Luther's pseudonym during his May 1521 to February 1522 exile in the Wartburg Castle under the protection of Frederick the Wise) "in present-day theology—also and above all in Catholic theology." ("Estado atual do entendimento" in *Lutero ontem e hoje, Concilium* 118:8 [1976]: 125; edition in Spanish, 292.)

offers for evangelical witness and life in the face of the challenges that Christians must confront in the present. This is the standpoint from which the following assessment proceeds.

The attempt to carry out such a project must of course also account for Luther's limits and his errors. Luther was no more a hero or an "evangelical saint" than he was a demon. Therefore, we should speak of those points in which Luther erred, was limited, or has been superseded. The following areas of controversy, here only briefly noted, are especially important in this regard:

1. In extra-church circles. Luther was in no way acritical in relation to authority. However, his almost general acceptance of the legitimacy of authority remains problematic, both theologically and in light of its historical effects, as does his position in favor of repression of the peasants.
2. In ecumenical circles. In recent years Catholic theology has expressed a broad acceptance of Luther's doctrine of justification. However, widespread controversy continues to characterize discussions about the *servo arbitrio* and the doctrine of the two kingdoms.[5]
3 Reservations expressed by Lutherans themselves. Erwin Mühlhaupt provides what is still a good summary of these reservations: Luther's vulgar speech; the lack of coherence in his willingness to give ecclesiastical power to the territorial princes, and in the reversal of his support for the peasants, leading to his call to the princes to put them down; his acquiescing in the persecution of the Reformed-Anabaptist movement in 1531 and 1536, and, toward the end of his life, in inciting the persecution of the Jews. Mühlhaupt also thinks there is an "imbalance" in Luther's use of Scripture and in the question of Holy Communion.[6] I would add to the list some incoherencies in the definitions Luther gives of the sacraments and his legitimation of infant baptism.[7]

These disputed matters and others deserve careful study and extended discussion. At this point, however, I propose two rather different tasks: first, to suggest an appropriate characterization of Luther and the

[5]See chapter 6.
[6]Erwin Mühlhaupt, "Was ist an Luther überholt und was nicht?" in *Luther* 41 (1970): 111–19.
[7]See Walter Altmann, "Sacramentos: Túmulo ou berço da comunidade cristã?" *Estudos Teológicos* 20:3 (1980):127–42.

movement that originated with him, and second, to offer a theological explanation for this characterization.

A General Characterization of Luther's Work

The movement that originated with Luther acquired four principal designations: Protestant, reforming, Lutheran, and evangelical. How relevant, how apt, is each of these terms?[8]

Protestant   In 1529, at the insistence of Emperor Charles V, the attempt was made at the Diet at Speyer to get the princes to retract the decision they had taken at the previous Diet in 1526, to allow evangelical territories to be constituted. Some princes protested, asserting that freedom of conscience was basic in questions of faith.

The term "Protestant" came to characterize Luther's movement, "becoming in time the 'secular' name of the adherents of the Reformation."[9] At Speyer—and in the life of Luther himself, at the Diet at Worms—protest was not simply for the sake of protest, but rather in the name of conscience.[10]

There appears to be a contradiction between this protest in the name of "conscience," on the one hand, and the "authoritativeness of Luther's doctrinal claim," on the other.[11] But it is not; it is an indispensable bipolarity. Nevertheless, this bipolarity of conscience and doctrine in Protestantism, taken as a contradiction, could explain the fact that within Protestantism both pietism and rationalism, each in its own way, cling to the conscience, while orthodoxy clings to the doctrine. Steck observes, in case we should understand this apparent contradiction as a dissociation: "In this case Luther's authority would carry within it the seed of its own dissolution."[12]

Luther knew that a conscience in turmoil could lead to desperation and self-annihilation; he also knew that a conscience freed by the Word

---

[8]In this part I am basically following Karl Gerhard Steck, "Die Autorität Luthers," in *Ecclesia semper reformanda,* a Festschrift for Ernst Wolf on his 50th anniversary (Munich, 1952), 104–120.

[9]Ibid., 116, quoting Ferdinand Kattenbusch. [All quotations from Steck translated into English from the German by the translator.]

[10]Ibid., 116.

[11]Ibid., *id.*

[12]Ibid., 117.

of God and bound to it had the duty, the courage, and the drive to protest. For Luther, then, the free conscience was tied to the Word of God. The conscience itself needs to go through a process of liberation, which is produced by justification, through the gospel.[13] "In other words: Luther's understanding of doctrinal authority does not exclude the prophetic element; it includes it."[14]

The term "Protestant" refers not simply to one who is against something, but to one who "*pro*-tests," that is, one who is in favor of some higher value. This interpretation is legitimate to the degree that as Protestants we are not simply contestants but also supporters of the gospel. To paraphrase Gustavo Gutiérrez, we might say that every "annunciation" implies a "denunciation," and every "denunciation" must serve "annunciation."[15]

The fact is, however, that Luther wanted to get to annunciation and stay there. Although the characterization "Protestant" may be valid to describe Luther's theology and the movement that took his name, it is probably not the most fitting term.

Reforming   Luther entered the history books as "the reformer," a designation appreciated even by the first evangelicals and mentioned in the Formula of Concord itself.[16]

In fact, a whole series of reforms was effected as a result of the preaching and the work of Luther. A church of the Reformation emerged; it was, Luther said, an *ecclesia reformata semper reformanda* (church reformed, always being reformed). But if the term "reforming" were the best characterization for Luther, "then the authority of the reformer would be the authority of the renewer or the innovator."[17]

Luther accused Rome of being the innovator, and defended himself against accusations of being innovative. On the contrary, he believed himself to be giving expression to the continuity of the true primitive church. For him, the dichotomy was not a static church versus a reformed church but rather the true church versus the false church. He never claimed to be reforming but simply to be preaching the gospel. According to Luther, it is the Word of God that transforms

---

[13]For analogous reasons Paul Tillich can talk about the "transmoral conscience," in *The Protestant Era* (Chicago: University of Chicago Press, 1965), 136ff.

[14]Karl Gerhard Steck, op. cit., 117f.

[15]Gustavo Gutiérrez, *Theology of Liberation: History, Politics, and Salvation,* rev. ed. (Maryknoll, NY: Orbis Books, 1988), 150–56.

[16]*The Book of Concord,* op. cit., 504.

[17]Karl Gerhard Steck, op. cit., 113.

reality: "The Word of God comes, whenever it comes, to change and renew the world."[18]

So the Reformation was for Luther the fruit of the preaching of the Word, not of Luther's plans. Luther was continually surprised by new events; the Lutheran movement that emerged was for him a great novelty. "Ingenuously," Luther said at a certain point, "I saw myself caught up by events."[19] The immediate and spectacular repercussions produced by the only modestly rigorous Ninety-five Theses offer a key illustration. Luther seemed to react to rather than induce events. This reactive disposition may explain some of the errors he made in his decisions with respect to political and social issues.

For Luther, the true church was God's creature, not a human construction. He wrote:

> Therefore they cannot tolerate the Word of God or those who declare it, for he [God] disfigures their building by causing cracks and rents in it. He is a rabble rouser who misleads the people whom they have so beautifully edified, ordered, and organized. His way of doing things is completely different from theirs.[20]

When he was accused of overthrowing the papacy without constructing a new church, he responded that constructing a church did not mean instituting new ceremonies; rather, he wrote, it meant "leading consciences out of doubt and murmuring and so on, into faith, knowledge, and certainty."[21] Luther wanted to proclaim the gospel, not to reform the church. The rest, he believed, was consequence.

Lutheran   Lutheran doctrine is (or should be)—obviously—Luther's doctrine. Appropriating Steck's formulation, there is an "indissoluble bond between person and cause in Luther's own doctrinal claims."[22] Luther could become very zealous about his doctrine and launch sharp polemics against those who disagreed with him. In elaborating his will in 1542, for example, he asked to be exempted from the formal, legal requirement that he be identified by the notary; he considered himself "a public figure, known both in heaven and on earth,

---

[18]*LW* 33:52.
[19]Steck, 114. [English translation by translator.]
[20]Steck, 114, quoting Luther, *WA* 31/I, 173; see *LW* 14:97.
[21]Steck, 114, quoting Luther *WA* TR III, no. 3323b; see *LW* 54:196.
[22]Steck, 118. [English translation by translator.]

as well as in hell, having respect or authority enough that one can trust or believe more than any notary. For as God, the Father of all mercies, entrusted to me, a condemned, poor, unworthy, miserable sinner, the gospel of his dear Son and made me faithful and truthful, and has up to now preserved and grounded me in it, so that many in the world have accepted it through me and hold me to be a teacher of the truth. . . ."

Therefore, he said, his own signature should suffice, of one "who is God's notary and witness in his gospel."[23]

But the designation Lutheran goes against Luther's express will: "I ask that men make no reference to my name; let them call themselves Christians, not Lutherans. What is Luther? After all, the teaching is not mine. . . . Neither was I crucified for anyone." Then he mentions I Corinthians 3, and calls himself a "poor stinking bag of worms," concluding: "I neither am nor want to be anyone's master. I hold, together with the universal church, the one universal teaching of Christ, who is our only master."[24] In another passage, Luther even says that the Word of God is being "profaned" with his name.[25] He makes it clear that he is aware of the distance between him and the Word of Christ.

How does this mesh with his doctrinal claims, which are bound up with his person as an instrument chosen by God? The response must be that to be Lutheran is an event, not a state of being:

> Therefore this advice is best of all: we should not suppose that the Gospel, which we now have, will stay with us forever. Wait, and see what the situation will be in twenty years. Then tell me about it again. After the death of the present pious and sincere pastors, others will appear who will preach and act according to the pleasure of the devil . . . The people become weary of the Word and suppose that it will endure forever. . . But it will come to pass that we will lose the Word; for it steals away unawares. . . .[26]

To be Lutheran is something that once acquired should not simply be preserved; it is a permanent task, carried out in continuously renewed fidelity to the gospel.

Here resides the truly problematic aspect of Lutheranism's confessional fixation, even in the sense of a particular church (Lutheran).

[23]Steck, 119, quoting Luther, WA Br 9, 573, 60–574, 68 and 71–72 (LW 34:297).
[24]LW 45:70–71.
[25]LW 45:70.
[26]Steck, op. cit., 120, quoting Luther WA 33, 417f (LW 23:262–63).

The assumption is that it is possible, with the person of Luther, to fix and in this way to preserve the contingent and instrumental identity of the evangelical cause. Blocking the "free course of the gospel" prepared the path for what Steck calls the "very problematic road from Luther to Lutheranism."[27]

Evangelical   The term evangelical seems to be the most appropriate characterization of Luther and his work. This term expresses "the authority of the cause, not of the human being."[28] It summarizes the fundamental interest Luther reiterated continuously, and explains his courage to protest. It describes the foundations of the Reformation—and perhaps, too, the contemporary relevance of Luther and by extension, of Lutheranism.

Luther's evangelical passion fueled his unceasing activity as a preacher. For him, the gospel came through the Word, the living, preached Word, in event and not in eternal fixation. The authority of the Word is "spiritual," understood as exempt from external coercion (through laws or governments) and internal coercion (through legal and doctrinal prescriptions articulated by ecclesiastical institutions).

Luther's own personal and public experience convinced him that in the event of proclamation the gospel always inspires anew. For him, the evangelical cause was a constant turn and return to the Word of God as expressed in the Bible.

What Does It Mean to Be Evangelical?

If evangelical is the term that most precisely characterizes the work and the intent of Luther, what would be central to what is understood as evangelical?[29] The many theologies of Luther reflect a tremendous disparity on this as well as on other questions.

---

[27]Steck, 119. [English translation by translator.]

[28]Ibid., 115. [English translation by translator.]

[29]Hans Küng in an interview once pointed out that the terms "evangelical" and "catholic," ordinarily used to designate church denominations, are really ecclesiologically complementary. What is evangelical, because it issues from the gospel of Jesus Christ, is at the same time necessarily catholic, in the sense that it has universal scope; it cannot be limited to one confessional body. Conversely, what is catholic, or universal, is only such if it is evangelical, that is, if it proceeds from and is in agreement with the gospel.

One of the basic characteristics of Luther's theology is its emphasis on Scripture and the exclusivity of Scripture as the source of doctrine and the faith. Luther's articulation of the principle of *sola Scriptura* (only through the Scripture) is most appropriately understood not as a determination of formal authority but as the discovery of a material center of Scripture, which at the same time serves also as an internal hermeneutical principle.

In expositions of a more popular cast, what is evangelical in Luther is often explicated in terms of the *solae* characteristics: *sola Scriptura, sola gratia, sola fide* (only through Scripture, only through grace, only through faith). Although this approach is consonant with the doctrine of justification, it is not always clear that these three principles, for their part, converge in the *solus Christus* (only Christ), who is above Scripture, the content of grace, and antecedent faith. Moreover, there is also a tendency to limit this exposition to the work of God in Christ for us and the appropriation of it by faith, forgetting the equally necessary new life of the believer.

Each theology of Luther presents its own structure, reflecting its author's perspective and presuppositions. There is no neutral theology, nor is there an abstract "universal theology of Luther." Our interpretations of Luther are inevitably influenced by our locations. We can and must take note, as much for ourselves as for our interlocutors, of our own motives and aims in studying Luther. This is not simply a matter of reproducing them, but rather of really interpreting them, of understanding them within the framework of our particular experiences.

The question, How to assess Luther? should converge with the question, What are *we* looking for when we assess Luther?

Justification by faith   The fact that it is common knowledge that this is Luther's central doctrine has not made it any less controversial, even within Lutheranism itself.

Justification by faith as a doctrine was, for Luther, the expression of a profound personal experience. (See chapter 2.) For the church, too, he argued, it was the fundamental doctrine, the article *stantis et cadentis ecclesiae* (on which the church stands or falls). Only when the preaching of the church is established on this article can that preaching break down pride and comfort the suffering. At the same time, the church, too, is tempted to try to merit the grace of God and to position itself between God and humanity as receiver of humanity's good works and transmitter of God's grace. Here is born the institutional security the church seeks and the authoritarianism that chokes it. Good works become works that the faithful do for the church. The church that lives in justification by faith, on the other hand, is the one that proclaims and freely transmits God's forgiveness.

What does the doctrine of justification by faith have to say to us today? Luther's juridical conceptualization is not easily accessible to people today, nor does his existential question arise automatically in everyone. Paul Tillich suggested one contemporary alternative when he argued that for twentieth-century human beings, the question of guilt and forgiveness might be replaced today by the question of emptiness and meaninglessness, overcome in unconditional acceptance.[30]

Implicit in the doctrine of justification is the rejection of values that prevail in modern societies—values in relation to production, possession, culture, power, and social stratification. Justified by faith, persons are accepted unconditionally as they are and not for what they have or can produce or even consume. To use Pauline terminology, the godless are justified. Here too is one of the important roots of the modern question of human rights, which should not be underrated among Lutherans as an expression of egotism, of the *amor sui* so criticized by Luther.

The doctrine of justification by faith is also critical with respect to the church itself, to the degree that the church is tempted to shape and accommodate itself to the values prevailing in its environment. There is always a danger that the church will make its decisions in accord with the accepted social morality. Its internal value system can become a copy of the model of economic production, and it can expressly (by identification) or tacitly (by virtue of the dichotomy) enter into alliances with the prevailing political power.

According to Luther's articulation of the doctrine of justification by faith, however, the church is as good as its hearing of the Word of God.

Evangelical freedom   The concept of evangelical freedom, as Luther presented it in *The Freedom of a Christian* (1520), has two

---

[30]See Paul Tillich, *The Courage to Be* (New Haven, CT: Yale University Press, 1952), 40–63, 155–78.

aspects.[31] In its first part, it is a variation on the doctrine of justification by faith. "A Christian is a perfectly free lord of all, subject to none," is the first thesis, which relates to the realm of faith.[32]

Basic to understanding this thesis is Luther's distinction between person and work.[33] From the outside, we can discern diverse works. We are inclined—Luther said we do it inevitably—to judge persons by their works. But works, Luther maintained, do not count before God. The believer is free.

> And when others challenge you with the passages in the Scriptures in which works have some value, stand fast with those that support grace. The passages that refer to works you should understand as treating works as consequences: live in grace and do not feel the lack of any merit; from there on in, the corresponding consequences will emerge.[34]

God wants to come before external works, to reach the person in his or her integrity. In the first commandment, according to Luther, God claims the whole person.[35] This is the basis of the peculiar freedom of Lutheran churches in relation to others whose peculiarity is their legalism. The "freedom of a Christian" is expressed in the joy of living and letting live, which in spite of many other deficiencies characterizes even today many Lutheran communities. Persons, the church, humanity—all need this freedom that in all systems, including the majority of ecclesiastical systems, is dramatically hidden.

But let us not get carried away. This is only half of the theme "Christian freedom." Luther's second thesis is that "A Christian is a perfectly dutiful servant of all, subject to all."[36] This applies in the sphere of love. Probably the greatest tragedy of Lutheranism, and its constant temptation, is to limit itself to the first thesis of Christian freedom. The other face of the coin is (should be): free *to serve*.[37]

---

[31] *LW* 31:333–77. The distinction Luther makes in this treatise between body and soul is not anthropological-biological (to establish the parts of the human being) but rather anthropological-relational (to establish the relationships of the human being). In the first part of the treatise, Luther refers to the relation of the human being with God, and in the second, to the relation of the believer with the neighbor.

[32] Ibid., 344.

[33] See Hans Joachim Iwand, *Glaubensgerechtigkeit nach Luthers Lehre* (Munich: Christian Kaiser Verlag, 1959), 47–50.

[34] *WA* 15, 424, 20–22. [English translation by translator.]

[35] Iwand, op. cit., 38–39.

[36] *LW* 31:344.

[37] In the quotation cited in n. 34, Luther refers to works as "consequences."

The good tree, in fact, produces good fruit.[38] Here, Luther does not hesitate to speak again of good works—in a positive sense. The same year in which he wrote his treatise on *The Freedom of a Christian* (1520), Luther also wrote a *Treatise on Good Works*.[39] Those works that used to be considered good, he argued—namely, those done for God and for the church (prayers, fasts, pilgrimages, penitences, veneration of relics)—were now decidedly evil. "For God and the church do not need" these works of the devil.[40] When the worship of God is reduced to works within the church, Luther wrote, it is the devil's doing. True good works are those that express service, love for one's neighbor.[41]

The Cross   This whole reversal is realized most decisively in the cross of Christ. Luther's *theologia crucis* renounces all triumphalism. The road to power is abandoned; only the path of weakness counts. At the cross, the point of convergence between God and the human being, the destiny of human life is turned around.

On the one hand, the cross signals the way of God who, abandoning majesty and terrible omnipotence, places God's own self in human hands, in an expression of divine love for human beings. Here is comfort for the believer: "The more we draw Christ down into nature and into the flesh, the more consolation accrues for us."[42]

On the other hand, the reality of God on the cross demolishes human pretensions of reaching God on its own or of establishing humanity itself as God. Christ assumes our sin—he becomes sinner; we receive his righteousness—and we become righteous.[43]

Justification costs God God's own son; it costs us our old selves. In what Luther defines as "conformity" with Christ, the believer's perspective begins to change.[44] Like Jesus, the believer does not orient him or herself toward those who are well but rather seeks out those who are ill; does not make alliances with the strong but rather seeks solidarity with the weak; does not see through the lens of the powerful but rather perceives from the standpoint of the oppressed.

---

[38]It is not simply that the tree "*should* produce good fruit," as Philip Melanchthon formulated it in the Augsburg Confession VI (*Book of Concord,* op. cit., 31). Emphasis added.

[39]*LW* 44:21–114.

[40]*WA* 10/I/2, 40. [English translation by translator.]

[41]Ibid., *id.*

[42]*LW* 52:12.

[43]See Iwand, op. cit., 63 (*"der fröhliche Wechsel"*).

[44]Ibid., 60.

For Luther's theological heirs, most especially for the churches that bear his name, this means that the essential point of reference is that of the "little ones," the weaker ones—"the least of these": sharecroppers, small farmers, employees, the unemployed, factory workers, immigrants, refugees, people of color, native peoples, women, children. If these "little ones" do not form the reference point for the church, then the church is not of Christ and, therefore, is neither evangelical nor Lutheran.

The new holiness   Finally, Luther changed the concept of holiness, shattering the double standard that prevailed in Catholic theology and practice.[45] The freedom justification by faith conferred permitted a radical reversal of values. So-called good works (veneration of relics, pilgrimages, purchase of indulgences, fasting, prayers, asceticism), Luther claimed, were practices of the devil. In the last analysis, they were done out of self-interest. (In spite of his polemic, however, Luther could accept and even require prayer, fasting, and discipline of the body as exercises in faithfulness toward God and as expressions of love for the neighbor.) On the other hand, those works that had been considered neutral or even "necessary evils," such as those aimed at material survival and social organization, Luther characterized as truly good works, desired by God. From the homemaker to the politician, professions were understood as vocations or "callings" and were recovered for holiness, for service to God and to the neighbor. Prostitution and usury, at the same time, were condemned as abuses of the human person and the neighbor and, therefore, of God. Those filled with apparent "holiness" were "sent empty away," whereas those "hungry" for the ethical were "filled with good things."

In Luther's time, this represented a complete reversal of values. Today, this same revolution must be reexperienced in radical new terms. In the consciousness of many evangelical Lutherans, this was limited—or so it appears—to the idea that one should be *efficient* in one's profession, and if one is a subordinate, one must be *obedient*. Surprisingly in practice efficiency negates justification by faith, which now becomes justification by professional efficiency—"whoever progressed did so because they worked"; furthermore, obedience negates

[45]See one of the classic articles of the Luther renaissance: Karl Holl, *The Reconstruction of Morality*, edited by James Luther Adams and Walter F. Bense, translated by Fred W. Meuser and Walter R. Wietake (Minneapolis: Augsburg, 1979 [original: 1919]).

freedom and the cross as perspectives and condemns the weak one to subordination, conformity, and slavery.

In order to understand the "new holiness" about which Luther wrote, we need to see it in terms of identification through the cross— identification of ourselves with those who are being crucified and, in turn, those we may be crucifying. We need to understand justification by faith as the freedom to take on the cross. This means that we must move beyond an understanding of "vocation" and "holiness" that is restricted to the secular professions. We must move toward a new, more ample definition, one that embraces those activities through which history is being made today.

Index of Persons

Index of Luther's Works